Creative
Dough Craft

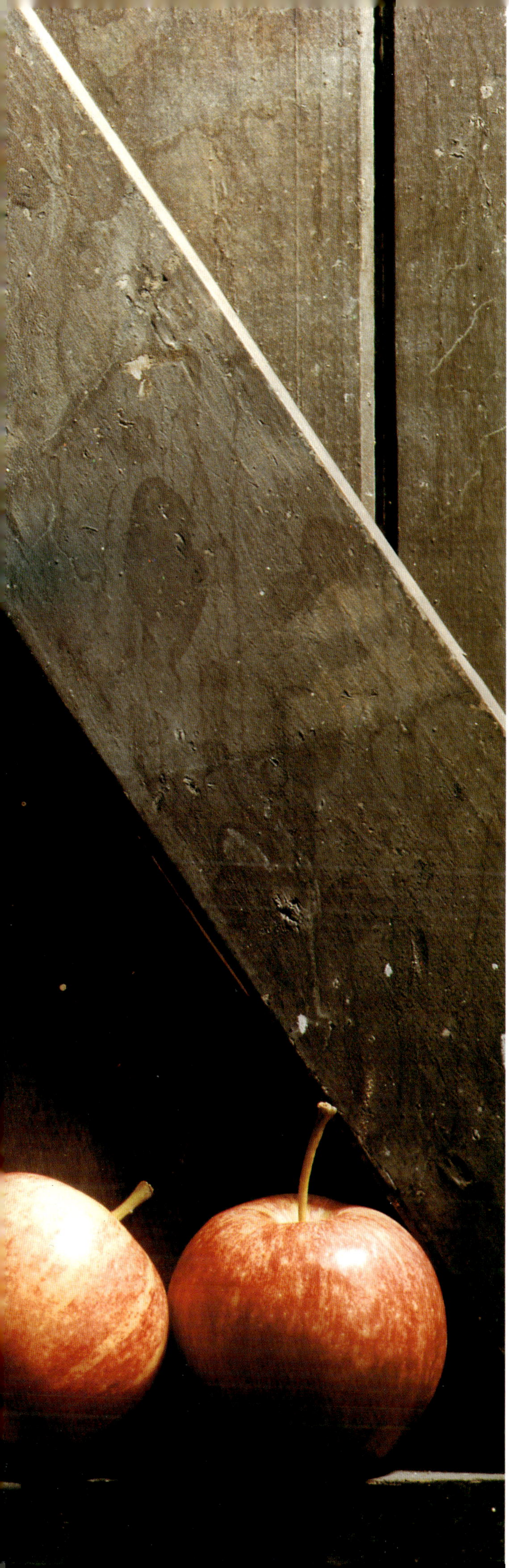

Creative Dough Craft

Over 40 original, innovative and traditional decorative projects to make from flour, salt and water

Cheryl Owen

Photography by Steve Tanner

Publisher's Note
Crafts and hobbies are great fun to learn and can fill many hours of rewarding leisure time, but some general points should be remembered for safety:

Always choose non-toxic material wherever possible, for example paints, glues, and varnishes. Where these are not suitable, use materials in a well-ventilated area and always follow the manufacturer's instructions.

Craft and kitchen knives, needles, scissors and all sharp implements should be used with care. Take special care with sharp materials, such as glass, metal and ceramics. Always cut onto a smooth, hard surface that will not be damaged, such as a chopping or cutting board.

Protect surfaces from paint, glue and varnish splashes by laying down old newspapers, plastic sheeting or an old sheet.

❤

Although salt dough is a good play medium for young children, remember that when baked, salt dough models can be heavy, and discretion should be used when allowing babies and young children to play with them.

This edition is published by Southwater

Distributed in the UK by
The Manning Partnership
251–253 London Road East
Batheaston
Bath BA1 7RL
UK
tel. (0044) 01225 852 727
fax (0044) 01225 852 852

Distributed in Australia by
Sandstone Publishing
Unit 1, 360 Norton Street
Leichhardt
New South Wales 2040
Australia
tel. (0061) 2 9560 7888
fax (0061) 2 9560 7488

Distributed in New Zealand by
Five Mile Press NZ
PO Box 33-1071
Takapuna
Auckland 9
New Zealand
tel. (0064) 9 4444 144
fax (0064) 9 4444 518

All rights reserved. No part of this publication may be reproduced, stored in a retrieval system, or transmitted in any way or by any means, electronic, mechanical, photocopying, recording or otherwise, without the prior written permission of the copyright holder.

Southwater is an imprint of Anness Publishing Limited
© 1995, 2000 Anness Publishing Limited

1 3 5 7 9 10 8 6 4 2

Publisher: Joanna Lorenz
Project Editor: Penelope Cream
Designer: Kit Johnson
Photographer: Steve Tanner
Stylist and Illustrator: Lucinda Ganderton

Contents

Introduction 6
Basic Techniques 8

♥

Decorative Touches
22

♥

Bowls, Platters & Containers
58

♥

Wall Ornaments
82

♥

Toys, Games & Animals
124

Templates 150

Index 158

Acknowledgements 160

Introduction

Salt dough is a surprisingly versatile and exciting craft medium. Much of its appeal lies in the simplicity of the procedure and the inexpensive and readily available ingredients needed – flour, salt and water.

The technique of modelling dough has a very long history, beginning with the Classical Romans, Greeks, and Egyptians, who all paid homage to their gods with offerings of figures moulded from dough. Salt dough modelling became very popular in Germany during the nineteenth century, when economical but highly effective Christmas-tree decorations were made from bread dough. Salt was added to the dough in order to prevent the ornaments from being eaten by mice. This was the start of a salt dough tradition in Europe, although the craft was lost during the First World War when salt was in short supply. Sadly, due to the fragile nature of the medium, few antique examples remain.

Children and adults alike will find plenty of inspiration for modelling with salt dough in the following pages.

~ ***Summer Pickings*** ~

This sheaf (left) and pretty flower basket (below) are both made in a traditional style, taking inspiration from the harvest.

~ Introduction ~

There are projects to suit all abilities, ranging from simple and effective motifs which can be stamped on to dough using pastry cutters, to more technically challenging three-dimensional creations.

The main techniques used throughout the book are covered in detail at the beginning, and easy-to-follow step-by-step instructions and photographs accompany each project.

~ *Floral Tributes* ~

The intricate pattern of the apple tree wreath (above) is well displayed in the natural dough surface. The circular theme is continued in the rosebud ring (above right) which uses roses in its border as can also be seen around the edges of the apple tree motif. Roses are used once again to decorate this unusual initial (right) which is the perfect customized gift.

~ Introduction ~

Basic Techniques

Modelling salt dough requires very little in the way of materials and equipment, and you will probably already have the basic items at home. You should work on a clean, smooth, flat surface, and take care to keep sharp implements, glues, paints, and varnish well out of the reach of children. Always try to use non-toxic materials wherever possible.

Salt dough is a marvellous modelling medium for children of all ages, as it is soft, non-toxic (even if toddlers try to eat the dough, they are unlikely to swallow it as it tastes so salty) and a lot of fun. However, when baked it does become hard and can be very heavy.

~ Simple Tools ~

Gathering the tools required for salt dough modelling is easy – for most of them you need look no further than the kitchen cupboard or the nearest craft shop. If you have an interest in kitchenalia, old wooden rolling pins, and antique moulds and cutters are always useful.

Hints & Tips

Making and Storing Salt Dough

Salt dough is made with plain (all-purpose) flour, not self-raising (self-rising) flour, water, and household table salt. The salt dough recipe appears on page 16, and is used throughout the book. Measurements are given in cups: as a guide, 1 cup of plain (all-purpose) flour weighs 3½ oz (100 g), 1 cup of salt weighs 7 oz (200 g) and 1 cup of water equals 7 fl oz (200 ml). The addition of 1 tablespoon (5 ml) of vegetable oil to the recipe will add suppleness, while 1 tablespoon (5 ml) of wallpaper paste can be added to give elasticity.

Salt dough can be prepared with an electric handmixer or a food processor with a kneading attachment, as a speedy alternative to making the dough by hand. The dough can be modelled immediately after making, but is best left to "rest" for 30 minutes, sealed in an airtight container. It is also important to keep dough that is not in use

~ *Rose Bouquet* ~

Natural, uncoloured salt dough holds detail very well, both when indented using a knife and, as here, when pressed into a flexible rubber mould.

~ Basic Techniques ~

~ *Marine Moulds* ~

Various objects can be used to give shape to salt dough. Here (left), a Victorian marzipan mould is used to produce little fish, while washed seashells or metal chocolate moulds produce equally effective designs (right).

sealed in this way so that it does not dry out. Salt dough can be wrapped in clear film (plastic wrap), although it will tend to become damp. The dough will keep for up to one week in an airtight container in the fridge, and should be taken out one hour before you intend to use it. If kept for a longer period the dough may become damp, and you will need to knead in a little extra flour.

Tinting Salt Dough

Food colouring is ideal for use on salt dough, and is available in liquid and paste form. The paste is easier to use, as it is less "wet" than the liquid. More than one colour can be added to the dough to produce the shade required.

Two or more different-coloured doughs can be combined by kneading to give beautiful marbled effects (see page 17). If a large amount of food colouring is used, extra flour may need to be added, as the dough may become damp. Varnishing baked, food-coloured models with polyurethane varnish instead of a water-based varnish will intensify the colour.

Using Templates

There are easy-to-use templates at the back of the book. These can be traced on to tracing paper and cut out to use as pattern guides. If a pattern is to be used a number of times, the template tracing should be transferred on to thin card. To do this, trace the template on to tracing paper, using a pencil, then place the tracing paper face-down on the card. Re-draw the motif on the back of the tracing and it will appear on the card.

Working with Salt Dough

The dough can be rolled out flat with a rolling pin. Work directly on to baking parchment (parchment paper), as this can then be slipped on to a baking tray when the model is ready to go into the oven. Large pieces can be modelled directly on to a small sheet of hardboard greased with cooking fat or vegetable oil – this will act as a releasing agent so that the dough does not stick to the surface.

A small, pointed knife, or clay-modelling tool is indispensible for cutting the dough and indenting details. A cocktail stick (toothpick), knitting needle or thick sewing needle is also useful and can be used to pierce holes for hanging or decorating models. Make any holes approximately 1/8 in (3 mm) wider than needed; this will allow for any distortion and for painting and varnishing.

Various heat-resistant materials make suitable moulds for modelling salt dough. Ovenproof bowls, plates and dishes, or shapes formed from card, should first be smeared with cooking fat or vegetable oil, which will act as a releasing agent. Thin card, baking foil, wire, and chicken wire can be shaped into armatures (supporting frameworks), which are then enclosed in salt dough. There is an exciting range of beautiful pastry moulds, biscuit (cookie) cutters, and delicate icing cutters available from kitchen shops and specialist cake-decorating suppliers. These are ideal for children and beginners to use.

~ Basic Techniques ~

slightly according to different ovens and the thickness of the dough. You should therefore refer to the baking times supplied as a guide only. Only when models are completely hard all over has the baking process finished. Turn off the heat and leave the model in the oven to cool. Models can be air-dried, although this will take a number of days.

Check models regularly for the first few hours of baking to see whether any air bubbles have appeared (this is due to the gluten in the flour). Pierce any air bubbles with a pin and gently depress the dough.

Any burrs on the surface of the baked dough can be sanded away with fine- or medium-grade sandpaper. Coarse-grade sandpaper is too rough, and should not be used. A nail file is useful for sanding intricate areas.

Painting and Finishing

Baked models can be left unpainted, although they must be varnished for protection. Paint can be applied directly on to the dough, or over an undercoat. Watercolour paints work successfully when painted directly on to salt dough, and different colours blend well on the surface due to the

~ *Egyptian Head* ~

Salt dough's natural tendency to crack can be put to excellent textural use. This "ancient" Egyptian head has been decorated in relief to emphasize the cracks. They add an antique air and lend authenticity to the design (above).

~ *Painted Finishes* ~

This vase piece (right) has been stippled to give the appearance of rustic porcelain, while the moulded salt dough shells are decorated in softer muted colours to give a realistic effect (below).

Textures

Experiment with creating various textures on the dough. Press it through a garlic press or sieve (sifter) to make spaghetti-like strands that are ideal for modelling hair or foliage, for instance, and decorate the surface of the dough with biscuit (cookie) cutters, nozzles, combs and many other items to produce interesting effects.

Baking Salt Dough

It is important to bake salt-dough models slowly and at a low temperature: 250°F/120°C/Gas ½. Although baking times are given for each project in the book, these will vary

~ Basic Techniques ~

12

~ Basic Techniques ~

porous nature of the dough. It is advisable to undercoat models before applying acrylic or craft paints, however, as this will prepare the surface and help to level out any unevenness. Household matt emulsion (flat latex) paint can be used for the undercoat, although acrylic gesso, available from art shops, is ideal. Gesso is more expensive than emulsion (latex) paint, but it dries very quickly and gives a thicker coverage.

Experiment with Indian inks and specialist craft paints which are now widely available from art and craft shops in exciting metallic and pearlized forms. The non-toxic and quick-drying qualities of many craft paints make them suitable for children to use.

A range of paintbrushes will be needed for different applications, from larger brushes for painting all-over colour to fine brushes for detailed work. Good-quality artist's brushes are worth the expense, and will give an excellent result. Special varnishing brushes made of badger's hair are recommended for varnishing, but a good-quality paintbrush will do.

It is vital to varnish finished models all over at least five times. Water-based varnishes dry quickly. Polyurethane varnishes take longer to dry and turn the surface slightly yellow, an effect that is often very effective, especially on objects painted with watercolour paints. Varnishes are available in gloss, satin and matt finishes. Fabric trimmings can be coated with PVA medium, which is available from art and craft shops. This will help to prevent the fabric from fraying.

Finally, remember that salt dough is susceptible to steam and damp, so always keep your creations in a dry atmosphere to prevent deterioration.

~ *Materials & Equipment* ~

Salt dough does not require any specialized equipment: all materials are easily obtained in either general art and craft stores, or around the home. Try experimenting with decorative devices such as glass "gemstones", metal ornaments and bent wire shapes – almost anything heatproof, in fact.

~ *Basic Techniques* ~

15

Salt Dough Recipe

Simply follow the method below to make the amount of salt dough you will require for each project. As a guide, the quantities given are enough to make a bowl about 9 in (23 cm) diameter.

INGREDIENTS

~

2 cups plain (all-purpose) flour
1 cup salt
1 cup water

1. Mix together the flour, salt and half the water in a mixing bowl. Knead the mixture, gradually adding more water until the dough has a smooth, firm consistency. Be careful not to add too much water or the dough will sag and become sticky.

2. Remove the dough from the bowl and continue to knead for 10 minutes. The dough can be modelled immediately, but is best left to "rest" for 30 minutes in an airtight container. Bake the salt dough in a domestic oven at 250°F/120°C/ Gas ½, until the model is completely hardened all over.

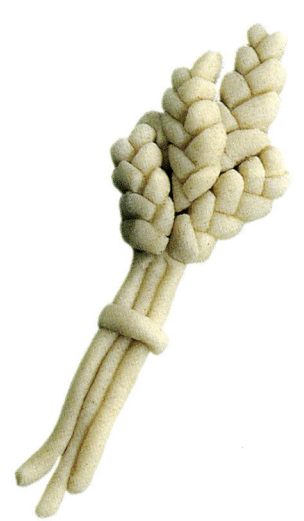

~ *Raw Dough* ~

Once the dough has been mixed, it is pliable and easily manipulated, suitable for even intricate details.

~ Basic Techniques ~

Simple Guidelines

TINTING AND MARBLING SALT DOUGH

1. Colour the dough with food colouring by adding a little colouring in a central dent. Fold the dough over and knead it thoroughly until it is evenly coloured, adding more colouring if necessary. To colour a large amount of dough, break it into small pieces and colour each one separately.

2. To marble the colours, roll differently coloured pieces of dough into sausages of equal size. Twist the sausages together and then knead the colours to blend them, being careful not to overdo the kneading or the veining effect will be lost. Try creating new colours by blending two shades together.

ROLLING OUT THE DOUGH

Roll salt dough out flat on to a lightly floured surface such as a chopping board, or on baking parchment (parchment paper) with a rolling pin. If the dough sticks to the rolling pin, sprinkle on a little flour.

~ *Basic Techniques* ~

USING TEMPLATES

1. If a template is to be used as a pattern for cutting the rolled-out dough, place it on the dough and cut around the circumference using a sharp knife or modelling tool. Remove the template and then gently pull away the excess dough around the image. Smooth the outer edges with the knife or modelling tool.

2. To create a rounded edge, gently pat the edge of the dough with a finger moistened in cold water. Any dough components which are to be joined together should first be moistened with a little water – the gluten content in the flour will then act as a natural glue. Be careful not to make the dough too wet, however, or it may sag and become sticky. Remember that water can stain the dough, so this will be a consideration if a model is to remain unpainted as every mark will be much more visible.

3. Transfer any details from the template to the dough by replacing the template and pricking along the lines with a pin. Remove the template and join the dots on the dough with a knife tip or other pointed implement such as a thick needle or cocktail stick (toothpick).

MAKING MOULDS

 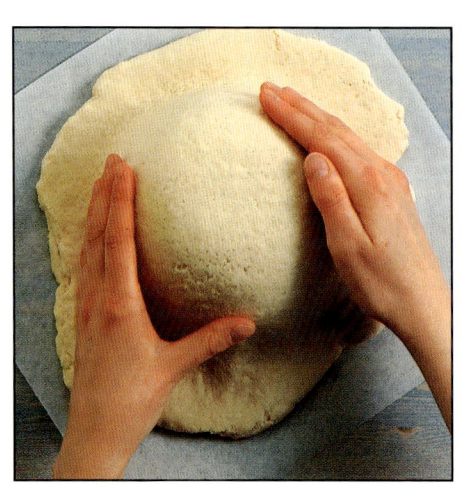 

1. Ovenproof plates, bowls and dishes can successfully be used as moulds. First smear the mould with cooking fat or vegetable oil – this will make it easy to remove the dough after baking. Roll the dough out flat to a thickness of approximately 5/16 in (8 mm) and large enough to cover the mould.

2. The dough should not be too wet or it will stretch when lifted, so sprinkle on a little flour to dry it if necessary. Carefully lift the rolled-out dough, supporting it underneath with your hand, and place it over the mould. Smooth the dough outwards from the centre, then cut away any excess dough.

~ *Basic Techniques* ~

ARMATURES (SUPPORTIVE FRAMEWORKS)

1. Sturdy card (cardboard) is useful for making armatures (supportive frameworks). If the card (cardboard) is to be curved, pull it smoothly across a scissor blade to round it more easily. Any joins should be stuck together with masking tape. The armature can be left in the model, but, if it is to be removed, smear it with cooking fat or vegetable oil before applying the dough so that it can be removed easily after baking.

2. Aluminium baking foil makes a very versatile armature for small models and components – simply crumple the foil and mould it to the required shape. Separate pieces can be joined together with masking tape. Spread the armature with salt dough, forming a layer approximately 1/4 in (5 mm) thick. The dough can then be built up and modelled in specific areas.

3. Large models can be supported with an armature of chicken wire. This will give strength to the models, making them less likely to sag and become distorted during the baking process. Squeeze the wire into shape and add separate pieces by hooking the cut edges together with pliers. Cover the armature with strips of baking foil, overlapping the edges and sticking with masking tape. Apply the salt dough on top to a thickness of at least 1/4 in (5 mm).

~ *Armature Dinosaur* ~

The outer coat of this dinosaur encases and is supported by a sturdy chicken wire and baking foil armature. The wire and foil are heatproof and so present no problems when it comes to baking the model.

~ Basic Techniques ~

EMBEDDING AND EMBOSSING

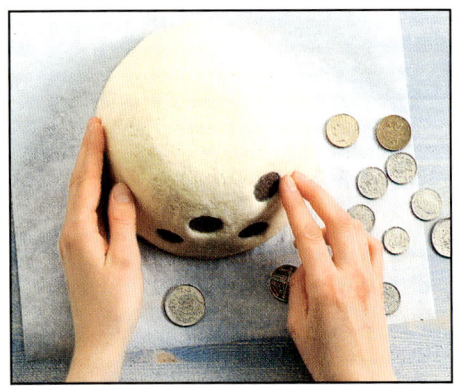

1. Various materials can be embedded into the dough, provided that they are ovenproof. Fragments of metal, wire, ceramic tiles, mirrors, shells and glass beads are all very effective. Press the object into the dough, then gently smooth the dough around the edges with a moistened finger.

2. Emboss the dough with textured objects such as buttons, lace or coarsely woven fabrics. An imprint can also be achieved by pressing wire or string into the dough. Press the object into the dough and remove it cleanly – make sure that the dough is not too wet or it will stick to the embossing implement.

BAKING SALT DOUGH

1. Sections of a model are often best baked separately first, or they may lose definition. This includes rounded shapes which are to sit in relief on a flat background. Bake the pieces for 1 hour, allow to cool, then moisten the undersides and spread sparingly with dough. Moisten the base piece and press the shape in place, then continue baking.

2. Some three-dimensional salt dough models which have been constructed over an armature cannot be covered with salt dough in one application. In this case, cover one side of the model and bake for at least 3 hours. Allow to cool, then apply dough to the other side, smoothing the new dough against the baked dough with a moistened finger.

3. When the top of the model is baked hard, it can be turned over or removed from its mould so that the underside can be baked evenly. After baking, turn off the heat and leave the model to cool in the oven. If necessary, sand away any burrs with medium-grade sandpaper. Finish sanding lightly with a fine-grade sandpaper until the model is smooth.

~ *Basic Techniques* ~

DECORATING AND PROTECTING SALT DOUGH

1. If you wish to paint the model with a dense, even colouring, it is advisable to undercoat the model first. Use either acrylic gesso or matt emulsion (flat latex) paint. Leave to dry, then paint the model with acrylic paints. Watercolour paints look effective applied directly to the dough, and can be blended first on a ceramic tile or old plate.

2. When the paint has dried, the model must be varnished. This is a very important stage. Leave any model which has been painted with watercolour paints to dry for at least 6 hours, as the water-thinned paints will sink into the porous dough. Varnish the model at least 5 times all over, allowing the varnish to dry between each coat. Use a fine brush to apply varnish into any pierced holes or intricate corners.

3. All is not lost if a model breaks. Repair unpainted and unvarnished salt dough models which have broken by moistening the surfaces to be joined. Smear with a little dough and press together, then bake the model for about 1 hour. Repair painted and varnished objects with wood glue or a hot glue gun.

~ *Painted Plate* ~

Dense colours are easy to apply and the shades remain bright once painted on.

~ *Fragile Horses* ~

Small models often crack but don't worry – repairs are easy and can be well disguised.

~ Basic Techniques ~

21

Decorative Touches

Salt dough sculpture works well on either a small or a large scale to provide an immense range of ornaments, festive decorations, jewellery, and useful home or office items. Whether forming bright spikes or gentle curves, the ornamental scope of salt dough is vast. Salt dough holds colour extremely well, allowing for the application of detailed paintwork, touches of gold, and the combination of ribbons, jewellery fittings and even coloured sugar "glass".

~ Ornate Array ~

All these wall pieces, plaques, items of jewellery, and masks provide a striking example of the versatility of salt dough. Few modelling mediums can produce such a wide variety of applications, especially where each displays a different decorative technique.

Tree Plaques

Create a menagerie of appealing creatures to decorate your home during the festive season. Salt dough tree decorations were very popular in nineteenth-century Germany, and they are just as appealing today - as well as being a great deal cheaper and much more original than the shop-bought variety. All your friends will soon want some too.

YOU WILL NEED
~

tracing paper and pencil
scissors
1 quantity salt dough (see page 16)
rolling pin
baking parchment (parchment paper)
small, sharp knife
ruler
fruit corer
drinking straw
baking tray
fine-grade sandpaper
watercolour paints
paintbrushes
ceramic tile or old plate
metallic craft paints
polyurethane satin varnish
ribbon

1. Scale up the plaque, pyramid and animal templates on page 150 to the size required. Transfer to tracing paper and cut out the shapes. Roll the dough out flat on baking parchment (parchment paper) to a thickness of approximately ¼ in (5 mm). Place the templates on the dough and draw round them with a knife to cut out the plaques. Carefully indent the broken lines with the tip of the knife.

2. From the remaining rolled-out dough, cut strips ¼ in (5 mm) wide for the frames, using a ruler to keep the edges even. Moisten the tops of the plaques and then place the strips along the outer edges, mitring the ends where they meet at the corners. Place the pyramid and animal templates on the remaining dough and cut out the shapes. Cut the head off the cheetah. Pat all the cut edges to round them. ▶

~ *Tree Plaques* ~

Each salt dough animal is modelled in relief on a flat plaque. Alter the shape and colours of the frames for variety.

~ Decorative Touches ~

3. Mould a diamond shape for the camel's ear. Moisten the ear and press it on to the head, indenting it with the knife tip. Moisten the cheetah's head and press it on to the body, overlapping the "neck". Moisten the dolphin's fin and press it in place. Mould a tiny triangle of dough for the cheetah's nose, dampen it and press in position. Indent the facial features and other details.

4. From the rolled-out dough, use a fruit corer to cut 4 circles. One circle will be the sun on the cheetah plaque. Punch a hole in the centres of the remaining circles with the end of a drinking straw. Moisten the tops of the plaques and press the circles in place.

5. Transfer the pieces, on the parchment, to a baking tray, and bake in the oven at 250°F/120°C/Gas ½ for 1 hour. Remove the pieces and allow to cool. Moisten the outer edges of the plaques with cold water and smear with dough to even out the surface. Be sure not to add too much water or you will begin to blur the edges rather than simply smoothing them.

6. Moisten the undersides of the pyramid, animal and sun shapes. Smear them with dough, then moisten the tops of the plaques. Press the pieces gently in place on the plaques. Return them to the oven and bake for a further 9 hours. Allow to cool, then lightly sand the edges usuing a fine-grade sandpaper to smooth away any burrs.

~ *Tree & Wreath* ~

Christmas provides an excellent opportunity for salt dough modelling, whether in the shape of a decorated tree with gifts added in relief (above), or as a more formal wreath in natural dough with painted ornaments (right).

7. Paint the models with watercolour paints, mixing the colours on a ceramic tile or old plate. Use a fine paintbrush to highlight the stars on the camel plaque with metallic paints. Apply 5 coats of satin varnish, allowing the varnish to dry between each coat. Thread ribbon through the rings to hang up the plaques.

~ Decorative Touches ~

~ *Decorative Touches* ~

Window Ornaments

These stylish decorations catch the light beautifully when hung in front of a window, as they twist and turn gently in any passing breeze.

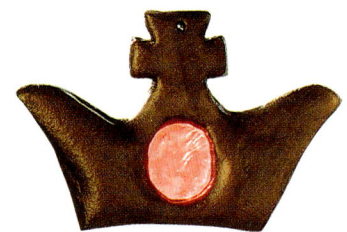

The wonderful stained-glass effect in the centre of the models is created from melted boiled sweets (candies) of various colours.

YOU WILL NEED

~

tracing paper and pencil

scissors

1 quantity salt dough (see page 16)

rolling pin

baking parchment (parchment paper)

small, sharp knife

extra flour, for dusting

boiled sweets (candies)

cocktail stick (toothpick)

baking tray

acrylic gesso or matt emulsion (flat latex) paint

paintbrushes

gold craft paint

water-based satin varnish

fine gold cord

1. Size the templates on page 150, transfer to tracing paper and cut out. Roll the dough out flat on baking parchment (parchment paper) to a thickness of 5/16 in (8 mm). Place the templates on the dough and cut out, using a sharp knife. Lightly dust with flour and place a boiled sweet (candy) in the centre. Cut around the sweet (candy), adding a 1/16 in (2 mm) margin. Remove the sweet (candy) and lift out the dough.

~ *Window Ornaments* ~

The boiled-sugar centres to these window ornaments give the impression of stained glass, glinting in the sunlight within deep gold surrounds. Gold cord hangers add to the luxurious richness of the ornaments (right).

2. Pierce a hole at the top of each shape with a cocktail stick (toothpick). Transfer the models, on the parchment, to a baking tray, and bake in the oven at 250°F/120°C/Gas ½ for 9 hours. Remove the models and, with the parchment still underneath, place a boiled sweet (candy) in each hole. Return the models to the oven for 30 minutes, then set aside to cool, leaving the sweet (candy) to set.

~ Decorative Touches ~

28

3. Undercoat the dough with acrylic gesso or matt emulsion (flat latex) paint, and allow to dry. Paint the shapes with gold craft paint, and allow to dry. Apply 5 coats of satin varnish, allowing the varnish to dry between each coat. Hang the models from gold cord.

~ *Fleur-de-lys & Star* ~

The combination of "gemstones" and pearlized craft paints add a lavish appearance to these hanging decorations. Their smooth surface takes the opalescent paint extremely well.

~ Decorative Touches ~

29

Classical Collection

Bird baths and Roman columns and vessels provide a classical theme for these "ancient" earrings, brooches and stick-pins. Salt dough lends itself well to jewellery-making, being fairly light and yet strong once it has been baked and varnished. These models have been decorated using quite a variety of materials and techniques, including embedding and embossing.

YOU WILL NEED
~
ceramic and mirror tiles
old towel
hammer
paper and pencil
scissors
1 quantity salt dough (see page 16)
rolling pin
baking parchment (parchment paper)
small, sharp knife
fine gold wire (optional)
button or pastry wheel
bonsai wire (available from garden centres)
small, round-nosed pliers
wire-cutters
stick-pins
baking tray
Indian inks
paintbrushes
water-based satin varnish
strong craft glue
brooch backs
kidney earring wires or clip-on earring backs
pendant hangers and drop beads

1. To make an embossed urn, wrap the tiles in an old towel and smash with a hammer into tiny fragments (throw the towel away after). Draw simple templates and cut them out. Roll the dough out flat on baking parchment (parchment paper) to a thickness of ¼ in (5 mm). Place a template on the dough and draw around it with the tip of a knife. Place some broken tile pieces within the shape then smooth the dough over the tile edges with a moistened finger. Cut out. Roll thin sausages of dough for handles; bend, dampen and press into place.

2. An alternative way of decorating a vessel shape is to add embossed patterning with a button or pastry wheel. The little bird shapes are made in a similar way, by cutting a shape and marking with a knife.

To make columns, cut out simple shapes in the usual way. To decorate, bonsai wire can be bent into a shape, then one end bent up at a right-angle to make a handle. Press the wire into the column to stamp a pattern. ▶

~ *Classical Collection* ~

The combination of embedded pieces of mirror and ceramic with Indian inks gives this collection the air of fragile porcelain.

~ Decorative Touches ~

3. Insert small wire loops into the earrings, from which to hang earring wires, dangle drop beads or join 2 models together (such as the bird-and-column earrings).

To make a stick-pin, push the pin into the dough. This design for a column shape was achieved with embossed tile pieces (as in step 1) and short strokes with the point of a sharp knife.

For all the pieces, bake in the same way: transfer to a baking tray, and bake in the oven at 250°F/120°C/Gas ½ for 7 hours. When cool, paint all the pieces with Indian inks, mixing in white to create pastel colours.

~ *Classical Suns* ~

Classical sources of inspiration are easy to find and often have clear imagery, making them easy to adapt for salt dough use. Here the ancient sun's face motif, a common image in classical Rome, is attached in relief to some colour washed wooden boxes. The motif is produced by means of pushing the dough into small circular moulds which have been greased with a releasing agent such as vegetable oil; this makes the dough shape easier to remove. Any extra details can be emphasized or added with the point of a knife.

4. To finish off, apply 5 coats of satin varnish, allowing the varnish to dry between each coat. Glue brooch backs to the brooches. Hang the earrings on earring wires or glue on clip-on earring backs.

To link the bird-and-column earrings, use small pliers to open the loops under the birds slightly. Slip these through the loops at the top of the columns, and close the bird loops again. Slip a pendant hanger through the loops under the column earrings, and squeeze the ends through the holes of the drop beads. If necessary, carefully squeeze the pendant hangers shut again using the small pliers. This should prevent the beads dropping off.

~ Decorative Touches ~

Grapes and Fallen Leaf Beads

Beads are easy objects to make from salt dough. Delicate, unusual shapes such as these pretty, luscious grapes and fallen leaves can be hung on fine wire loops and used to make jewellery, or applied as a finishing touch when caught in the seam of a small purse.

YOU WILL NEED

~

1 quantity salt dough (see page 16)
rolling pin
baking parchment (parchment paper)
small, sharp knife
small, round-nosed pliers
fine gold wire
wire-cutters
cocktail sticks (toothpicks)
baking tray
watercolour paints
paintbrushes
plastic clay
polyurethane satin varnish
thick thread
scissors
2 calotte crimps
necklace clip and jump ring

1. To make the bases for the bunches of grapes, roll three balls of dough ¾ in (2 cm) diameter on baking parchment (parchment paper). Mould each ball into an oval and flatten. Squeeze one edge to a point. Roll several small balls of dough for the grapes, then moisten each base with water and press on the grapes, taking care not to squash the balls out of shape.

2. To make the leaves, roll the dough out flat on baking parchment (parchment paper) to a thickness of ⅛ in (3 mm). Cut out leaf shapes with a small, sharp knife, and indent the veins with the tip of the knife. Pat the cut edges with a finger moistened in cold water to round and smooth them. Moisten the undersides of 3 leaves and press on to the bunches of grapes. ▸

~ Decorative Touches ~

 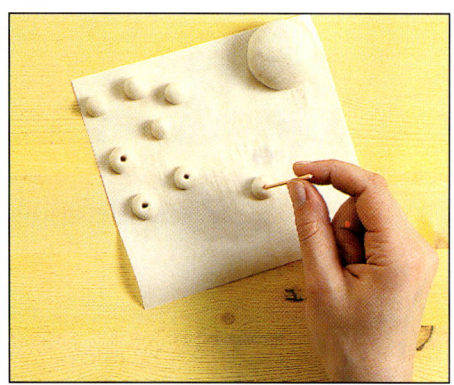 

3. Using small round-nosed pliers, bend the fine, gold wire to make a hanging loop, leaving a "stalk" ⅜ in (1 cm) long. Repeat to make 3 loops. Insert one stalk into the centre top of each bunch of grapes. Leave enough wire protruding to form the hanging loop, and try to leave an equal size loop on each bunch.

4. To make the round beads, roll out approximately 24 balls of dough, ⅝ in (1.5 cm) in diameter, for a necklace, and approximately 10 balls, ¼ in (5 mm) in diameter, for a bracelet. Pierce a hole in each bead with a cocktail stick (toothpick). Transfer all the pieces, on the parchment, to a baking tray, and bake in the oven at 250°F/120°C/Gas ½, removing the leaves and round beads after 6 hours and the grapes after 8 hours.

5. Leave to cool, then paint with watercolour paints, blending two autumnal colours together on the leaves. Round beads can be slipped on to cocktail sticks (toothpicks) for painting, inserted into plastic clay to dry. Apply 5 coats of satin varnish, allowing the varnish to dry between each coat, and, using a small paintbrush, apply varnish inside the bead holes and over the bases of the loops.

6. Thread one bunch of grapes on to a length of thick thread, positioning it in the centre, and make a knot on either side. Add a round bead on either side, knot, and then add the 2 remaining bunches of grapes. Add the rest of the beads in a pleasing design, knotting the thread occasionally to anchor them. Knot the thread against the end beads.

~ *Chestnut Leaves* ~

Natural objects make excellent transfers for salt dough. The dough surface is soft enough to pick up tiny veins on leaves, as here where an impression has been taken from a horse chestnut sprig. To make a similar model, simply press the sprig on to thinly rolled dough and remove gently.

7. Make a tight knot ⅜ in (1 cm) from the last bead on each side, and cut the excess thread close to the knot. Enclose each end knot in a calotte crimp and close tightly with the round-nosed pliers. Join the calotte crimps to a necklace clip at one end and a jump ring at the other. To alter the length of the string of beads, simply make more leaf and grape shapes.

~ Decorative Touches ~

~ Autumn Leaves ~

Repeated shapes are easy to produce from salt dough, as it cuts easily even around curved contours. These leaves are decorated in pleasantly muted watercolours, the shades blending smoothly from yellow to green.

~ Grapes and Fallen Leaf Beads ~

All these beads are made from salt dough, from the bunches of grapes to the delicate red yellow ovals along the top of the drawstring bag. They are light and easy to wear and, once varnished, quite durable.

~ Decorative Touches ~

Venetian Masks

A stunning carnival mask modelled from coloured salt dough can be decorated with a variety of exotic materials. Here, ribbons, *dried roses and iridescent beads have been used to great effect, but you could of course use any other decorations that you like.*

YOU WILL NEED
(to make 1 mask)

~

½ quantity of salt dough
(see page 16)
egg-yellow food colouring
pencil and paper
scissors
masking tape
ovenproof dish
baking foil
cooking fat or vegetable oil
rolling pin
small, sharp knife
13 in (33 cm) of ⅜ in (1 cm)
diameter wood dowelling
yellow Indian inks
paintbrushes
polyurethane satin varnish
sheer ribbons
thread
all-purpose household glue
small iridescent beads
dried roses
old lace

1. Colour the salt dough following Step 3 on page 17. Use the templates on page 151 to cut a mask and nose panel from paper, and cut out the eye holes. Stick the nose panel to the mask with masking tape, matching the dots.

2. Tape the mask to an upturned rounded dish. Mould a piece of baking foil to fit under the nose panel and stick it to the dish with masking tape. This foil mould will remain supporting the mask "nose" during the baking process. Remove the mask and smear the dish and "nose" with cooking fat or vegetable oil to allow it to be released easily later on. ▶

~ *Venetian Masks* ~

Two beautiful masks modelled on the Venetian carnival style. The final decoration can be as elegant or as frivolous as desired. The delicately moulded flowers on the lower mask are also made from salt dough, forming a superb three-dimensional frieze.

~ Decorative Touches ~

3. Roll the dough out flat to a thickness of approximately 5/16 in (8 mm). Carefully lift the dough and place it over the greased mould. Position the paper template mask on top and cut out the shape in the dough. Cut out the eye holes. Remove the paper template. Pat the cut edges with a moistened finger to round and smooth them. Bake the mask in the oven at 250°F/120°C/Gas ½ for 4 hours. Allow to cool. Remove the mask from the mould.

4. Roll a sausage of coloured dough, moisten it and press to the underside of the mask along one side. Press the end of the dowelling on top and smooth the dough over it, enclosing the end of the dowelling. Return the mask to the oven for 5 hours. Allow to cool, then paint the dowelling handle with sunshine-yellow Indian ink. Apply 5 coats of satin varnish, allowing the varnish to dry between each coat.

5. Arrange ribbons on the mask, tying tightly with thread to gather the ribbon in places. Glue the ribbons in place and cut the extending ends into chevrons. Glue iridescent beads over the threads to hide them. Cut the heads from the stems of dried roses and glue them to the mask. Highlight areas of the mask with a few more beads glued at random. Alternatively, decorate the mask with lace strips and coloured-dough shapes such as flowers.

~ *Flower Garland* ~

Realistic flowers such as those modelled along the top of the carnival mask on the previous page are effective in both natural and painted dough. The petals can be rolled in a variety of thicknesses and then curled to produce the flower shapes.

~ Decorative Touches ~

Wheatsheaf

The wonderful golden colour of baked dough lends itself beautifully to the theme of a sheaf of wheat.

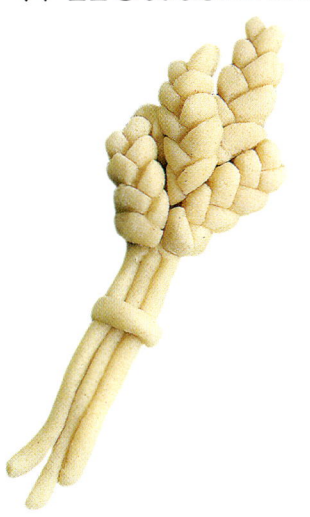

The model makes an ideal decoration for a kitchen wall, but keep away from steam.

YOU WILL NEED

~

pencil and tracing paper

scissors

1 quantity of salt dough (see page 16)

rolling pin

baking parchment (parchment paper)

small, sharp knife

modelling tool (optional)

baking tray

polyurethane satin varnish

paintbrush

1. Size the template on page 151, transfer to tracing paper and cut it out. Roll the dough out flat on baking parchment (parchment paper) to a thickness of 3/8 in (1 cm), and use the template to cut out the wheatsheaf shape. To make the stalks, roll out thin spaghetti-like strands of dough to a length of about 4¾ in (12 cm) and build them up into a bundle as shown. Moisten the strands with a little water to prevent them from drying out.

2. To make the tie for the bundle, roll 4 strands to a length of 4¾ in (12 cm). Join the ends together at the top, using a little water, and gently separate out the strands. Lay the first strand over the second, and the third over the fourth. Then lay what is now the third strand back over the new second strand. Repeat these 2 steps until the braid is complete. Pinch the bottom ends together, using a little water to moisten and stick in place. ▶

~ Decorative Touches ~

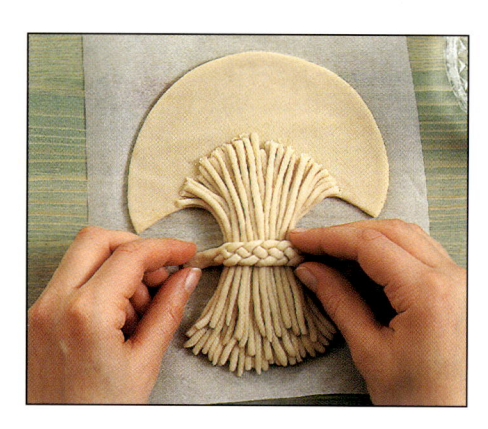

3. Moisten one side of the braid and carefully position it over the bundle of stalks at the narrowest point. Tuck the ends of the braid neatly underneath to conceal them. If they are too long to tuck under completely, trim slightly with the point of the knife.

4. To make the ears of corn, roll sausages from the remaining dough, each measuring 1¼ x ⅜ in (3 x 1 cm). Taper the rolls at one end and flatten them slightly. Use a knife or modelling tool to mark separate grains, curving the edges of each one. The finished sheaf will need up to 50 individual ears.

5. Dampen the outer edge of the wheatsheaf base and gently press on the first row of ears. Build up the other rows in overlapping layers. Transfer the model, on the parchment, to a baking tray, and bake in the oven at 250°F/120°C/Gas ½ for 10 hours. Apply 5 layers of satin varnish.

~ *Wheatsheaves* ~

The finished wheatsheaf (right), baked and varnished to a rich golden colour. Poppies are added to the bundle of ears of wheat in this pretty sheaf (left). The flowers have been picked out in red while the rest of the model remains unpainted.

~ Decorative Touches ~

40

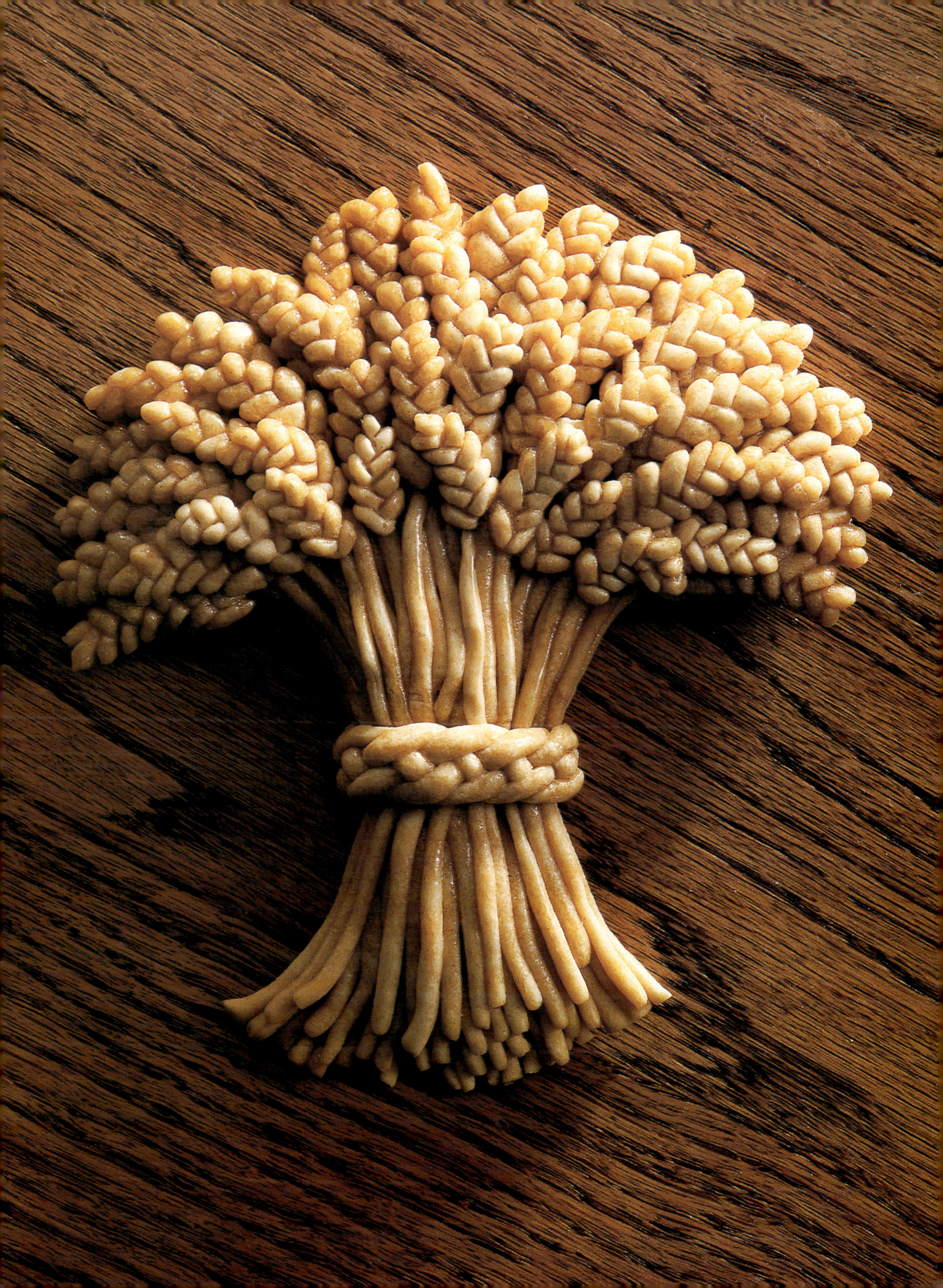

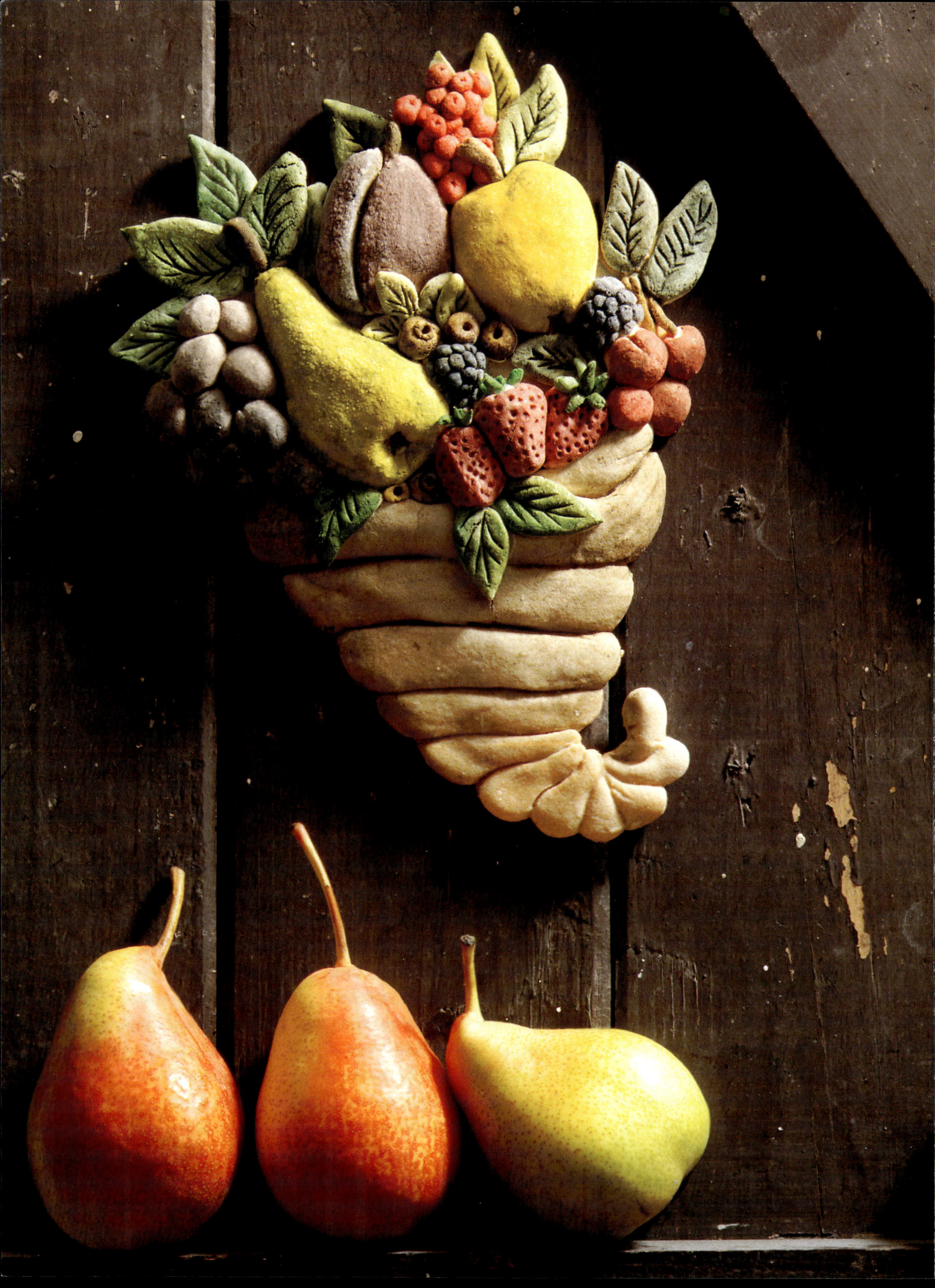

Fruit-Filled Cornucopia

This spectacular cornucopia, overflowing with fruit of every kind, is well worth the time that it takes to make. The realistic touches, *such as the individually moulded blackberries and seeds on the strawberries, make the fruit look almost good enough to eat.*

YOU WILL NEED

~

pencil and paper

scissors

2 x quantity salt dough
(see page 16)

rolling pin

baking parchment
(parchment paper)

small, sharp knife

dressmaking pin

modelling tool

knitting needle

2 cloves

eyelet loop

baking tray

watercolour inks

paintbrushes

polyurethane matt varnish

1. Size the template on page 151, transfer to paper and cut it out. Roll the dough out on baking parchment (parchment paper) to a thickness of 5/16 in (8 mm). Place the template on the dough, cut it out, and transfer the pattern by pricking with a pin. Use a modelling tool to define the ridges on the cornucopia.

2. Shape a pear, plum and apple from the remaining dough, following the template patterns. Moisten the undersides with water and gently press the fruit into place. Shape the leaves, marking the veins with the tip of the knife, moisten and press in position, being careful not to squash them out of shape. ▶

~ *Fruit-Filled Cornucopia* ~

A wealth of dusky, painted fruit seems to burst from the natural dough base. This harvest cornucopia follows the traditional salt dough theme of natural objects used to decorate the home.

~ Decorative Touches ~

43

3. Mould the grapes individually by rolling small balls of dough and then elongating them slightly. Moisten the base with water and apply the grapes.

Make the 2 blackberries from 1/8 in (3 mm) pellets of dough, applied individually to a 3/8 in (1 cm) foundation ball. Moisten the base and gently place the blackberries in position. Make the cherries and nuts from 1/2 in (1.25 cm) balls of dough, indenting the nuts with the point of a knitting needle.

4. Make the redcurrants from 5/16 in (8 mm) round berry shapes, and mark each with a tiny cross using the knife tip. Form 3/4 in (2 cm) balls of dough into a conical shape to make strawberries, and add a stalk at the top of each. Use the knitting needle to mark seeds on the surface. Moisten each shape as you make it, and press into position.

Make stalks for the cherries, apple, plum and pear from small rolls of dough, and insert a clove into the bases of the apple and pear.

5. Cut out the final 4 leaves, moisten them and attach to the underside of the cornucopia. This gives extra depth to the model. Press an eyelet loop into the back of the model so that it can be hung up. Transfer the model, on the baking parchment (parchment paper), to a baking tray, and bake in the oven at 250°F/120°C/Gas 1/2 for 20 hours. Allow to cool, then paint with watercolour inks. When dry, apply 5 coats of matt varnish, allowing the varnish to dry between each coat.

~ *Decorative Touches* ~

~ *Rose Bowl* ~

This model uses the combination of painted flowers on a natural dough base. The roses are modelled from sheets of dough, with veined leaves added between the blooms. The handles on the bowl have been indented using a modelling tool and, like the base, have been varnished but left their natural dough colour (left).

~ *Spring Basket* ~

This pretty posy uses painted flowers with a natural "container". The basket is literally woven from strips of salt dough, placed in a lattice over a flat support. The basket is left unpainted while the assorted flowers, including roses, forget-me-nots, lily-of-the-valley and daisies, have been picked out in colour (below).

~ Decorative Touches ~

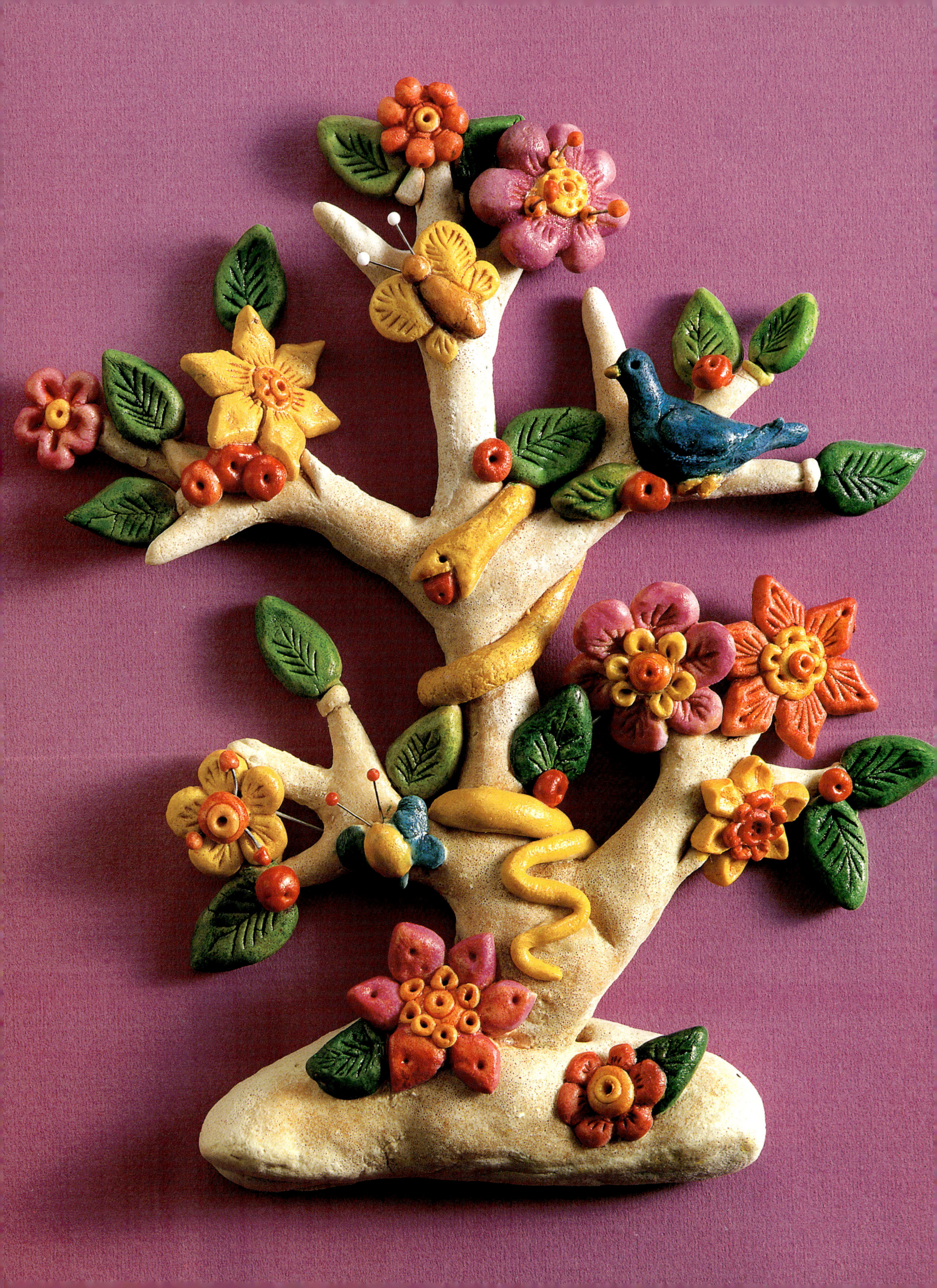

Mexican Tree of Life

This wonderful model looks very complex, but is in fact quite straightforward – although a little time-consuming – to make. The tree itself is left unpainted both to make it look natural and to contrast with the assortment of bright flowers and exotic creatures on its branches.

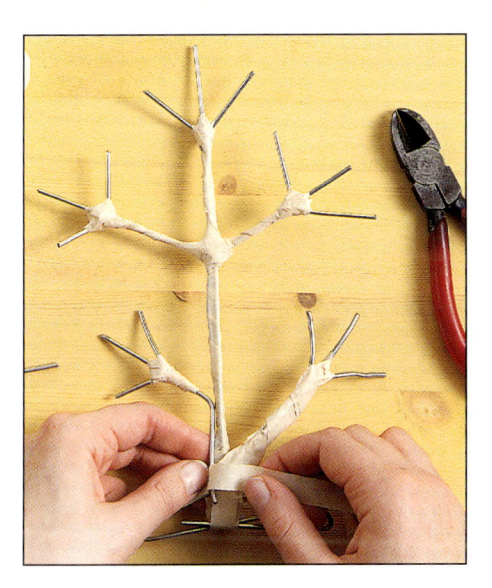

1. The tree is built up over a wire armature which supports its branches during and after baking. Make this from lengths cut from a coathanger with wire-cutters, bound together with pieces of narrow masking tape at the joins.

YOU WILL NEED

~

wire coathanger
wire-cutters
narrow masking tape
baking parchment (parchment paper)
1 quantity salt dough (see page 16)
small, sharp knife
knitting needle
medium-weight wire
glass-headed dressmaking pins
baking foil
baking tray
watercolour inks
paintbrushes
satin and matt polyurethane varnish

2. Working on baking parchment (parchment paper), cover the wire armature with a layer of dough, shaping the ends of the branches into points, but ensuring the dough is still forming a thick enough layer to cover the wire fully. Smooth over the joins with a moistened finger. ▶

~ *Mexican Tree of Life* ~

This Tree of Life is based on the brightly coloured Mexican models emblazoned with multi-layered flowers and various species of wildlife. Here there is a biblical serpent with the apple in its mouth, and birds and a bee and butterfly complete with pin antennae.

~ Decorative Touches ~

3. Form the serpent from a roll of dough, tapered towards one end. Cut a small slit at the head end and insert a pea-sized apple into the open mouth. Mark the eye with a knitting needle, moisten the dough and coil the serpent around the tree trunk.

4. Shape individual leaves on to short lengths of wire, indenting the leaf surfaces slightly with a modelling tool and marking the veins with a knife tip. Insert the wires into the dough of the branches, securing each with a small collar of dough.

5. Build up the flowers petal by petal. Roll small balls of dough, pinch them into diamond shapes and then press together, using a little water. Decorate the centres with small balls of dough and indent the petals using the knitting needle.

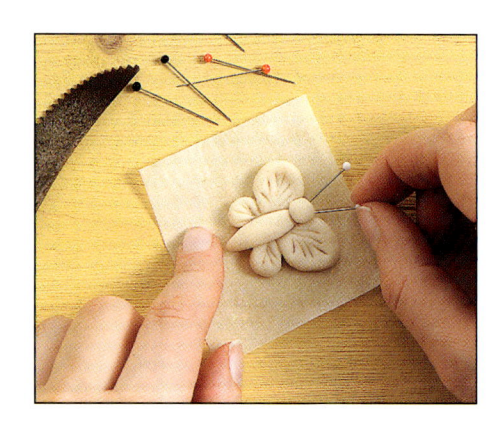

6. Make the bee and butterfly by rolling small round heads and sausage-shaped bodies. To make the wings, roll small balls of dough and flatten them slightly. Moisten with water and gently press on to the bodies. Use glass-headed dressmaking pins as antennae.

~ *Vase of Flowers* ~

Salt dough flowers can be made in various ways. In the Mexican Tree of Life, they are built up petal by petal. Other methods involve a single layer of petals, as here, or thin sheets of dough carefully curled around each other.

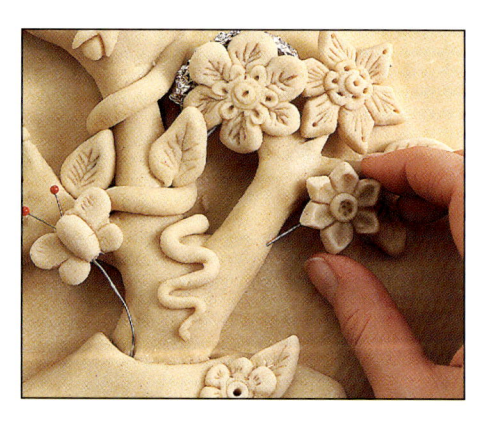

7. Attach the flowers and insects to the trunk with short wire stalks. Make a dove of peace if you wish, following the picture as a guide. Place small pads of baking foil under the flowers to help the tree to remain three-dimensional while it is baking. Transfer the model, on the parchment, to a baking tray and bake at 250°F/120°C/Gas ½ for 10 hours. Allow to cool, then paint with watercolour inks, leaving the trunk unpainted. Coat the painted areas with 5 coats of satin varnish and the trunk with 5 coats of matt varnish.

~ *Decorative Touches* ~

Bead Necklace

These beads can be decorated and painted to suit your own personal style and taste. Make a matching bracelet to go with the necklace, and use salt dough to make other exciting fashion accessories such as rings, earrings and pendants. Once varnished, salt dough is fairly strong and is therefore ideal for producing jewellery especially as it can be shaped into so many designs.

YOU WILL NEED

~

chopping board and flour for dusting (optional)
baking parchment (parchment paper)
1 quantity salt dough (see page 16)
small, sharp knife
paintbrushes
stick or skewer
baking tray
acrylic gesso or matt emulsion (flat latex) paint
acrylic or craft paints
polyurethane matt varnish
coloured cord

1. Working on a lightly floured chopping board or baking parchment (parchment paper), make a selection of as many beads as you like. Make each bead by moulding a small piece of dough in the palm of your hand and then flattening it to a greater or lesser extent depending on the shape required. Decorate the beads with indentations using the tip of a knife or the end of a paintbrush, or add on small pieces of dough, using a little water to make them stick.

2. Make a hole through the centre of each bead using either a stick or a skewer. The holes should be large enough to allow the coloured cord used later for threading to pass through each bead, but not so large that they cause the beads to lie in a crooked fashion once threaded. Transfer the beads on baking parchment (parchment paper) to a baking tray and bake in the oven at 250°F/120°C/Gas ½ for 8 hours until hard. ▶

~ Decorative Touches ~

3. Remove the beads from the oven and leave them to cool. Paint each bead with an undercoat of acrylic gesso or matt emulsion (flat latex) paint and leave to dry. Decorate the beads with acrylic or craft paints in your chosen designs and leave to dry. Apply 5 coats of matt varnish, allowing the varnish to dry between each coat.

4. Thread the beads on to a piece of coloured cord that is long enough to go over your head, and tie a knot to secure.

~ *Bright Rings* ~

Salt dough rings are simple to make: mould bold shapes and bake until hard, then paint in bright, contrasting colours and stick on to a ring base using a strong, clear glue (below and right).

~ *Bead Necklace* ~

The patterns of salt dough beads can be bright and varied. Here, lumps of dough add texture and bumps that can be individually coloured. The designs can be as outrageous or as classical as you wish; exuberant colours sit in contrast one on top of the other, or sometimes in bright stripes. The varnish helps prevent chipping and the necklace will prove durable and fun to wear (right).

~ Decorative Touches ~

~ Decorative Touches ~

Crown Letter Rack

This brightly painted letter rack would make a cheerful addition to any desk or table. Design and make your own original range of desk-top objects from salt dough to co-ordinate with the letter rack, such as boxes or the pencil holder shown on page 55.

YOU WILL NEED

~

1 quantity salt dough (see page 16)
rolling pin
chopping board and flour for dusting (optional)
baking parchment (parchment paper)
pencil and paper
scissors
small, sharp knife
paintbrush or similar implement
baking tray
fine-grade sandpaper
acrylic gesso or matt emulsion (flat latex) paint
acrylic or craft paints
polyurethane satin varnish

1. Roll the dough out flat on a lightly floured chopping board or baking parchment (parchment paper) to a thickness of 1 in (2.5 cm). Draw 3 crown shapes and a base shape to the size required. Transfer to paper and cut out the shapes. Place the paper templates on the dough and cut around them carefully with a knife.

2. Roll 9 balls of dough, each about 5/8 in (1.5 cm) in diameter, and then flatten them. Moisten the points of the crowns with a little water and press the flattened balls in place. Make small indentations on the balls using the end of a paintbrush or a similar-shaped implement. Transfer the pieces, on baking parchment (parchment paper) to a baking tray, and bake in the oven at 250°F/120°C/Gas 1/2 for 5 hours.

~ Decorative Touches ~

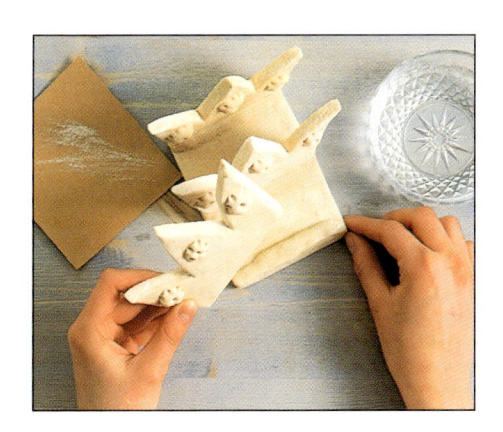

~ *Crown Letter Rack* ~

Although this letter rack is painted in a variety of contrasting colours, a more sedate version could be produced either in colours to match an office or study, or to emphasize the regal theme: the crowns' bases could be deep red or purple, and the edge painted in glittering gold.

3. When the pieces are cool, sand them down so that all the edges are smooth. Attach each crown to the base using a strip of tacky salt dough and smooth down with a moistened finger so that the joins are not noticeable. Place the letter rack back in the oven for 2 hours until all the joins have hardened.

4. Give the letter rack a final sand down so that it is really smooth. Paint on a coat of gesso or matt emulsion (flat latex) paint and leave to dry before decorating with your own choice of paints. When dry, apply 5 coats of satin varnish, allowing the varnish to dry between each coat.

~ Decorative Touches ~

Pencil Holder

Add this useful pencil holder to the crown letter rack to create the ultimate in desk organization and style. The holder is quick and easy to make, and can be painted in any number of colours and designs to co-ordinate with your other desk-top accessories.

YOU WILL NEED

~

cardboard paper-towel tube

scissors

1 quantity salt dough (see page 16)

chopping board and flour for dusting (optional)

baking parchment (parchment paper)

baking tray

biscuit (cookie) cutter

acrylic gesso or matt emulsion (flat latex) paint

paintbrushes

acrylic or craft paints

polyurethane satin varnish

~ **Pencil Holder** ~

This tubular design can be adapted for many uses other than just a pencil holder. A larger version can be constructed for use in the kitchen to hold wooden spoons and other utensils (take care to store only dry objects in dough containers, however). The tube design is ideal for keeping children's wax crayons tidy (far right).

1. Cut the paper-towel tube to a 4¾ in (12 cm) length. Roll the dough out flat on a lightly floured chopping board or baking parchment (parchment paper) to a thickness of ⅜ in (1 cm). Use the dough to cover one half of the tube, smoothing the surface with a moistened finger. Transfer the tube, on baking parchment (parchment paper), to a baking tray, and bake in the oven at 250°F/120°C/Gas ½ for 30 minutes. Cover the remaining half of the tube with dough, smoothing down any visible joins with a moistened finger.

2. Return the tube to the oven for another 30 minutes. To make the base of the holder, re-roll the remaining dough to a thickness of approximately ⅜ in (1 cm). Cut out a shape using a biscuit (cookie) cutter, transfer it, on the baking parchment (parchment paper), to a baking tray, and bake it in the oven with the tube at 250°F/120°C/Gas ½ for 8 hours until hard.

When both the tube and base are cool, smear them with dough and join them together, smoothing down the joins with a moistened finger.

~ Decorative Touches ~

3. Roll out 6 sausages of dough, long enough to fit round the tube, and attach them around the holder using a dab of water to help them stick. Roll 6 small balls of dough and stick them around the opening rim, again using a little water. Return to the oven for another 5 hours.

4. When the pencil holder is cool, paint on an undercoat of acrylic gesso or matt emulsion (flat latex) paint and leave to dry. Paint the holder with acrylic or craft paints to co-ordinate with your other desk equipment, and leave to dry. Apply 5 coats of satin varnish, allowing the varnish to dry between each coat.

~ *Decorative Touches* ~

Spiky Napkin Rings

These eye-catching napkin rings will enliven any table setting – paint the rings to co-ordinate with your china and table-linen. Individual names can be painted on the underside of each ring so that no one gets their napkins muddled up! The coats of varnish mean that the rings are easily wiped clean.

YOU WILL NEED
(to make 1 napkin ring)

~

cardboard tube

scissors

*½ quantity salt dough
(see page 16)*

rolling pin

*chopping board and flour for
dusting (optional)*

*baking parchment
(parchment paper)*

baking tray

*acrylic gesso or matt emulsion
(flat latex) paint*

paintbrushes

acrylic or craft paints

polyurethane matt varnish

1. Cut the cardboard tube to a 2½ in (6 cm) length. Roll the dough out flat on a lightly floured chopping board or baking parchment (parchment paper) to a thickness of approximately ¼ in (5 mm). Slightly dampen the tube with a little water and cover it inside and out with dough, smoothing down all the joins with a moistened finger.

2. To make the spikes, roll 9 balls of dough, each with a diameter of approximately 1 in (2.5 cm). Narrow one end of each ball to make a point, and flatten the other end. Transfer the spikes and the ring, on baking parchment (parchment paper) to a baking tray, and bake in the oven at 250°F/120°C/Gas ½ for 45 minutes until hard.

~ **Spiky Napkin Rings** ~

These unusual napkin rings jazz up a table (right); make a set specially for a party or celebratory dinner. The colourways can be altered according to the occasion: bright and colourful for a children's party or summer picnic, or perhaps pretty pastel tones for a wedding or formal lunch.

~ Decorative Touches ~

~ *Table Chic* ~

Try decorating the napkin rings in contrasting tones and picking out details, such as the points of the spikes, with dots of colour and wavy bands (below).

3. Remove the pieces from the oven and, when cool, smear both the spikes and the ring with dough and stick on the spikes. Smooth down any visible seams with a moistened finger and return to the oven for a further 9 hours and bake until firmly joined.

4. When the napkin ring is cool, lightly sand it all over. Paint on a coat of acrylic gesso or matt emulsion (flat latex) paint and leave it to dry before painting on your own colours and designs. When dry, apply 5 coats of matt varnish, allowing the varnish to dry between each coat.

~ *Decorative Touches* ~

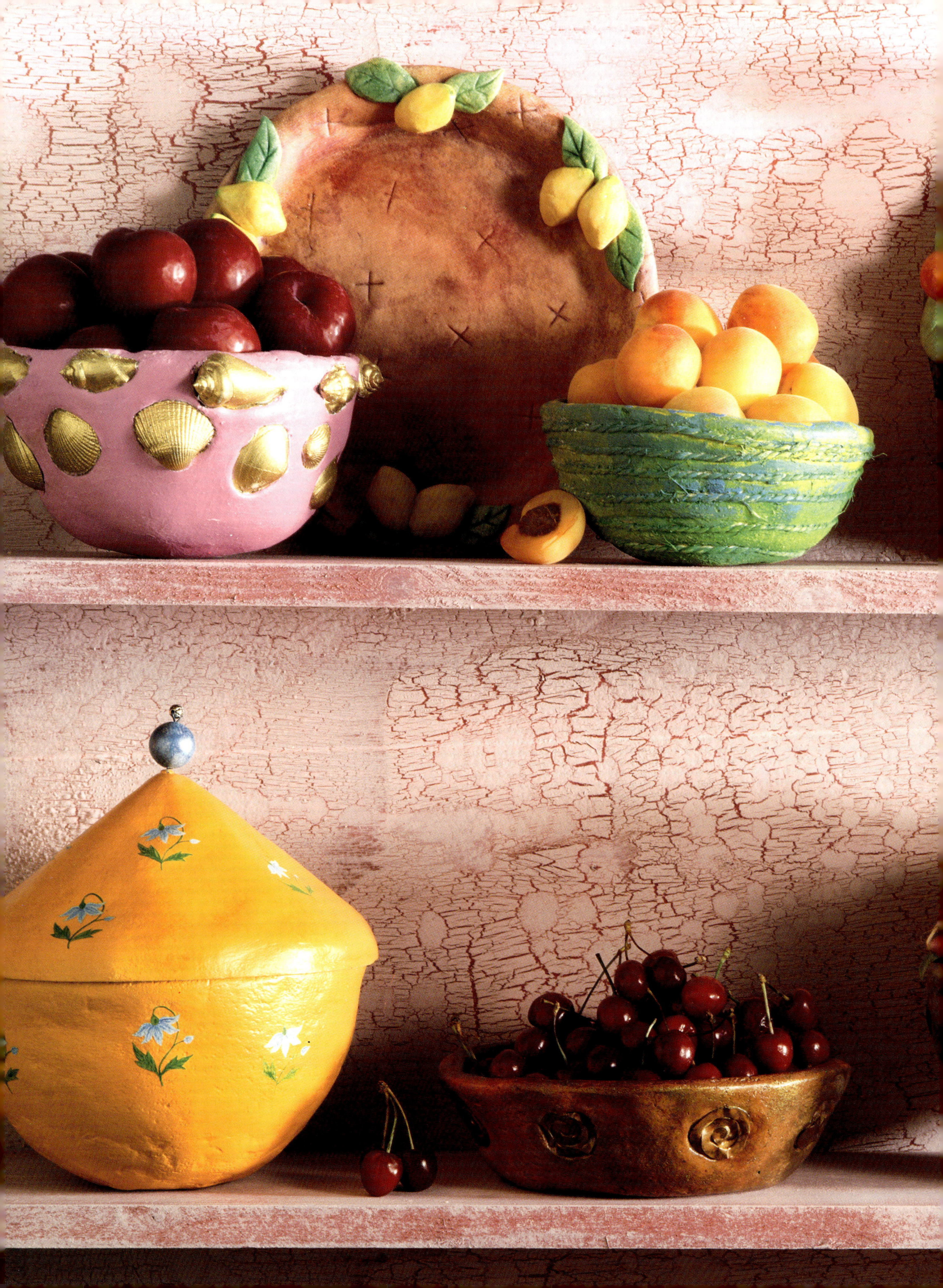

Bowls, Platters & Containers

Perfect for presentation and display, for holding trinkets, fruit, nuts and candies, an incredible range of dishes, plates, and bowls can be produced easily using salt dough. The versatility of the dough means that highly individual pieces can be created, with dramatic use of shape and decorative techniques. All manner of objects can be used as moulds to form the container, and the shape and function can be changed with the addition of rims, handles, and lids. Strips and balls of dough produce a variety of textures and raised designs, and can be altered to suit taste and decorative style.

~ Bowls of Plenty ~

All manner of bowls and containers can be created by moulding salt dough over different-shaped dishes or armatures. Flat platters can be built up as you work, and decorated in an infinite number of original designs.

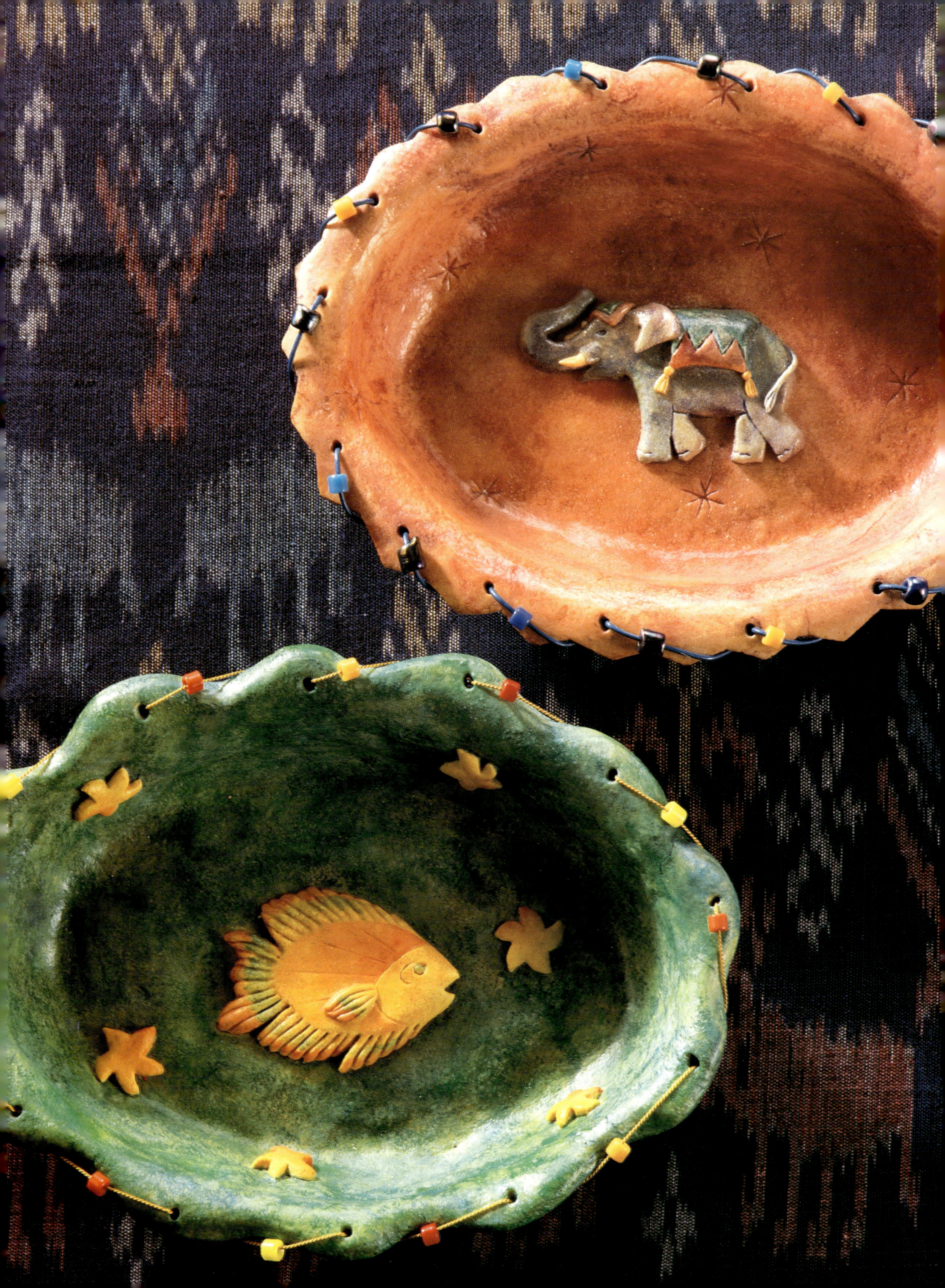

Elephant and Fish Dishes

These richly detailed dishes are decorated with appliqué-style motifs and would make a delightful addition to any setting. The holes around the rims are made before baking, and the little beads are threaded through at the end to add a colourful touch.

YOU WILL NEED
~

oval ovenproof dish with a rim
cooking fat or vegetable oil
1 quantity salt dough (see page 16)
rolling pin
baking parchment
(parchment paper)
small, sharp knife
skewer
tracing paper and pencil
scissors
baking tray
watercolour paints
paintbrushes
ceramic tile or old plate
polyurethane satin varnish
plastic or leather thonging
beads

~ **Elephant and Fish Dishes** ~

These creative containers, made using standard ovenproof pie dishes as moulds, are transformed into innovative bowls with clever rim designs. Draw templates of your own to produce a variety of appliqué effects.

1. Smear the inside and rim of an ovenproof dish with cooking fat or vegetable oil. Roll the dough out flat on baking parchment (parchment paper) to a thickness of 5/16 in (8 mm). Carefully lift the dough into the dish, and gently press in place. Using a sharp knife, cut off the excess dough around the edge, then cut a zig-zag pattern on the rim. Pierce holes around the rim with a skewer. Indent stars over the surface at random, using the tip of the knife.

2. Scale the elephant template on page 153 to the size required and transfer to tracing paper. Cut out the elephant, blanket, ear and head-dress. Roll the remaining dough out flat on baking parchment (parchment paper) to a thickness of 1/4 in (5 mm), place the templates on top and cut out the components. Pat the cut edges with a moistened finger to round them. Moisten the blanket and head-dress and place them on the elephant. ▶

~ Bowls, Platters & Containers ~

3. Roll a thin sausage of dough for the tail and stick in place. Gently indent the end of the tail with the knife. Moisten the head, then place the ear in position and smooth it on to the head with a moistened finger.

~ *Moulded Fish* ~

The fish theme can be adapted to provide free-standing ornaments that make intriguing decorations on their own. Here, a cooking mould rather than a flat template is used, and the fish is then coloured in blending, muted tones.

4. Indent the details and the eye with the knife. Roll a thin tusk, and squeeze one end to make a point. Moisten the head and position the tusk, bending the tip upwards. Roll a small ball of dough and press it over the wide end of the tusk. Transfer the elephant, on the parchment, to a baking tray, and bake it and the dish in the oven at 250°F/120°C/Gas ½ for 1 hour. Allow to cool, then moisten the underside of the elephant and smear with dough. Moisten the centre of the dish and press the elephant in place.

5. Return the dish to the oven for 12 hours, removing the mould during baking when the top of the dough has hardened. Paint the dish with watercolour paints, blending the colours on a ceramic tile or old plate. Apply 5 coats of satin varnish, allowing the varnish to dry between each coat. Lace the thonging through the holes, threading on a bead between each hole. Knot the ends together under the rim. Adapt these instructions to make a fish dish, using the fish template on page 153 to make the central motif.

~ *Bowls, Platters & Containers* ~

Metal-Embedded Bowls

These rustic bowls have the appearance of weather-worn stone. The heat-resistant qualities of metal provide an exciting source of decorative materials to use with salt dough – here, coins, bronze decorations intended for making jewellery, wire, and copper motifs have been embedded in the dough.

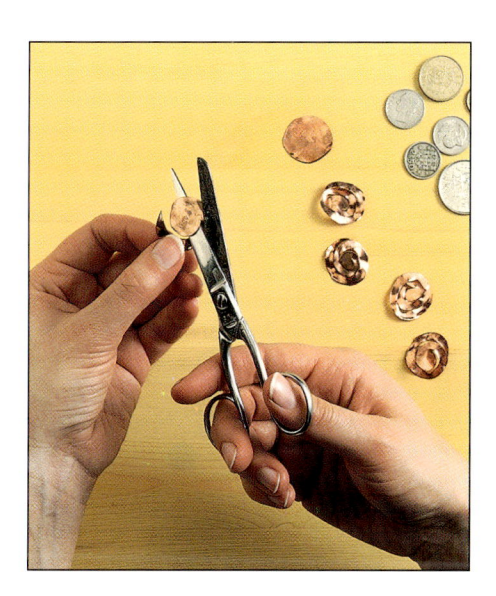

YOU WILL NEED
(to make 2 bowls)

~

2 ovenproof bowls

cooking fat or vegetable oil

2 x quantity salt dough (see page 16)

rolling pin

baking parchment (parchment paper)

small, sharp knife

fine copper sheet (available from craft shops)

old scissors (to cut copper)

metal for embedding, e.g., metal jewellery accessories, bonsai wire (available from garden centres), coins

pair of compasses, pencil and paper

baking tray

ruler or tape measure

watercolour paints

paintbrushes

metallic craft paints

natural sponge

polyurethane satin varnish

jewellery stones

all-purpose household glue

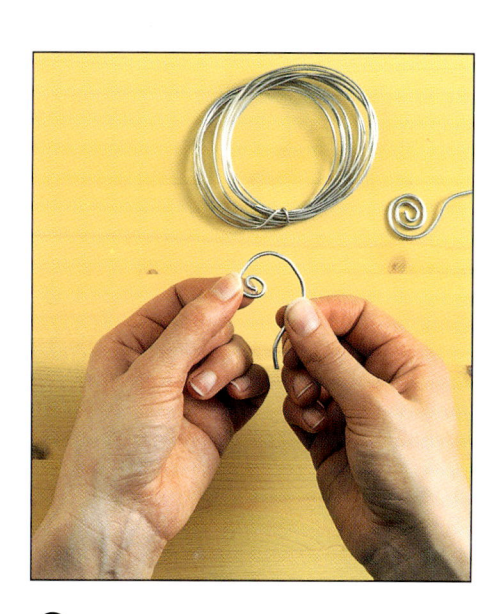

1. Smear the upturned bowls with cooking fat or vegetable oil. Divide the dough in half and roll each piece out flat on baking parchment (parchment paper) to a thickness of ³⁄₈ in (1 cm). Carefully lift each piece of dough and place it over a bowl, smoothing it down. Cut the edges level, using a knife. To make spirals of copper, cut rough circles from a sheet of thin copper using old scissors, then cut the circles into spirals. Press your chosen metal pieces into the dough. Bake in the oven at 250°F/120°C/Gas ½ for 9 hours, removing the bowls during baking once the dough has hardened sufficiently.

2. To make a flat lid, draw a circle on paper ¾ in (2 cm) larger all round than the dough bowl, using a pair of compasses. Cut out the circle to use as a template. Roll the remaining dough out flat to a thickness of ³⁄₈ in (1 cm), and use the template to cut a circle. Roll a ball of dough, moisten it and press to the centre. Smooth the edges to join it to the lid. Coil two lengths of bonsai wire and bend the ends downwards to form two halves of a heart for the handle. ▶

~ Bowls, Platters & Containers ~

3. Insert the metal handle ends into the centre of the lid. Transfer the lid, on the parchment, to a baking tray and bake in the oven at 250°F/120°C/Gas ½ for 5 hours, until it is almost hardened. Measure across the dough bowl between the inner edges. Using the pair of compasses, draw a circle on paper with a diameter of ⅜ in (1 cm) less than that of the measurement. Cut this out and use as a template to cut a circle from rolled-out dough.

4. Upturn the baked lid and support it on the ovenproof bowl. Moisten the back of the lid and place the smaller circle on top. Return to the oven for 5 hours until completely hardened.

5. Paint the bowls and lid with water-colour paints, blending your chosen colours together and adding black or white to dull the colours. Lightly dab the bowls with metallic craft paints, using a natural sponge. Wipe any paint off the metal before it dries. Leave the bowls to dry, then apply 5 coats of satin varnish, including the metal decorations and base of the handle, allowing the varnish to dry between each coat. Glue jewellery stones to the metal decorations.

~ *Bowl Collection* ~

This crinkle-edged bowl (above) is moulded around a small dish and then the edges are crimped and furled by hand. The outside edges can be streaked with paint as here, or decorated with all manner of embedded metal objects (right).

~ Bowls, Platters & Containers ~

~ Bowls, Platters & Containers ~

String and Shell Bowls

Make a range of bowls, using different-sized and shaped moulds and textures, remembering always to grease the mould with cooking fat or *vegetable oil before covering it with salt dough. For a more natural style, leave the bowls unpainted and apply a few coats of varnish for protection.*

YOU WILL NEED
(to make 2 bowls)

~

2 ovenproof bowls

cooking fat or vegetable oil

2 x quantity salt dough
(see page 16)

rolling pin

chopping board and flour for
dusting (optional)

baking parchment
(parchment paper)

shells

string

baking tray

acrylic gesso or matt emulsion
(flat latex) paint

paintbrushes

acrylic or craft paints

polyurethane matt varnish

~ *String and Shell Bowls* ~

The string and shell decorations, combined with bright tropical colours, turn plain containers into unusually exuberant fruit bowls, perfect as centrepieces on a dining table (right).

1. Smear the upturned bowls with cooking fat or vegetable oil. Divide the dough in half, and then roll each half out flat on a lightly floured chopping board or baking parchment (parchment paper) to a thickness of 3/8 in (1 cm). Carefully lift one piece of dough and mould it on to the outside of one of the bowls. Smooth the dough with a moistened finger and carefully cut away the excess dough around the edge. Repeat with the second bowl.

2. To decorate the shell bowl, select a variety of shells that will produce the decorative pattern you require. Wash the shells thoroughly with a mild detergent in warm water, and then press them gently into the dough. Smooth the dough around the shells with a finger moistened in cold water to help keep them in place. Do not press too hard or you may push the shells through the dough to the mould.

~ Bowls, Platters & Containers ~

3. To decorate the string bowl, start at the base and wrap the string around the bowl in a spiral shape, pushing it gently into the dough and smoothing it into place. Transfer the bowls, on the parchment, to a baking tray, and bake in the oven at 250°F/ 120°C/ Gas ½ for 12 hours. Allow to cool, then carefully remove the bowl moulds.

~ *Moulded Shells* ~

In the absence of real shells, imitation shells can be formed quite easily from salt dough. A copper Victorian chocolate mould, for example, produces defined contours and a realistic likeness (above).

4. Paint on an undercoat of acrylic gesso or matt emulsion (flat latex) paint and leave to dry. Paint the bowls and decorations with acrylic or craft paints, if you wish, or leave them unpainted for a natural look. Apply 5 coats of matt varnish, allowing the varnish to dry throughly between each coat.

~ Bowls, Platters & Containers ~

Citrus Fruit Plates

Oranges and lemons border these colourful plates to give a warm Mediterranean feel to their surroundings. The very realistic-looking fruits and leaves are easy to mould, and are painted with watercolour paints. A final coating of satin varnish creates the soft shine of healthy fruit and helps prevent chipping.

YOU WILL NEED

~

2 ovenproof plates, approximately 8½ in (22 cm) in diameter

cooking fat or vegetable oil

2 x quantity salt dough (see page 16)

rolling pin

small, sharp knife

baking parchment (parchment paper)

baking tray

watercolour paints

paintbrushes

polyurethane satin varnish

1. Smear the ovenproof plates with cooking fat or vegetable oil, so that the dough will be easy to remove after baking. Divide the dough in half, and roll each piece out flat to a thickness of ¼ in (5 mm). Carefully lift the dough pieces and place one over each plate. Cut away the excess dough with a small, sharp knife, and pat the cut edges to curve them. Reserve the trimmings.

2. Indent crosses at random on the dough, using the tip of the knife. Roll the remaining dough out flat to a thickness of approximately ¼ in (5 mm). Use the knife to cut leaf shapes – 12 leaves were used for each of these plates – and indent the vein pattern with its tip. Smooth along the edges of the bowl with a moistened finger to round them.

~ Bowls, Platters & Containers ~

3. Working on baking parchment (parchment paper), roll nine 1 in (2.5 cm) balls of dough for the oranges, and nine for the lemons. Squeeze the edges of the lemons at opposite sides to narrow them. Transfer the fruit and leaves, on the parchment, to a baking tray, and bake all the pieces in the oven at 250°F/120°C/Gas ½ for 1 hour. Remove the pieces and allow to cool. Moisten the undersides of the leaves and fruit, smear with dough and press to the rim of the plate. Bake for 9 hours, removing the plate mould when the top of the dough is completely hard. Paint with watercolour paints, then apply 5 coats of satin varnish, allowing the varnish to dry between each coat.

~ *Citrus Fruit Plates* ~

The fruity themes of these plates can be varied according to whim. Try experimenting with bunches of grapes, clusters of strawberries or blueberries. Vegetables, too, would provide attractive borders, especially highly coloured peppers or chillies, carrots and tomatoes.

~ Bowls, Platters & Containers ~

Tasselled Boxes

These subtly marbled boxes have been created using food colouring. Marbling is a simple technique which can produce a range of results and endless patterns, depending on how many colours are used and how thoroughly the dough is kneaded. Laced with cord and golden tassels, the boxes have many practical uses and could have matching lids.

YOU WILL NEED
(to make a small box)

~

1 quantity salt dough (see page 16)

egg-yellow and blue food colourings

rolling pin

baking parchment
(parchment paper)

small, sharp knife

ruler

drinking straw

baking tray

fine-grade sandpaper

books or weights

string

polyurethane satin varnish

paintbrush

gold cord

clear sticky tape

4 gold tassels

scissors

1. Divide the dough in half. Colour one half egg yellow and the other blue, then marble the colours together following the instructions on page 17. Roll the dough out on baking parchment (parchment paper) to a thickness of 5/16 in (8 mm). Using a knife and ruler, cut 4 squares of 4 x 4 in (10 x 10 cm) for the sides and 1 square of 3¾ x 3¾ in (9.5 x 9.5 cm) for the base. Punch a row of 5 holes with a drinking straw along 2 opposite sides of the larger squares.

2. Transfer the squares, on the parchment, to a baking tray, and bake in the oven at 250°F/120°C/Gas ½ for 5½ hours. Allow to cool, then sand the backs and sides of the squares. Moisten the cut edges of the base and smear with coloured dough. Moisten the lower edge of one square on the back and press it upright against the base. Support in place with a book or weight. Add another square in the same way beside the first. Smear coloured dough inside the box along the joins.

~ Bowls, Platters & Containers ~

~ Tasselled Boxes ~

The tasselled boxes work well as flower-pot or houseplant containers (below), but remember not to let them become damp when watering the plants. Make up decorative pebbles from any scraps of leftover marbled dough.

3. Add the other squares in the same way to complete the box, and tie string around it to hold the sides in place. Return to the oven for 2 hours. Allow to cool, then smear more dough along the joins under the base and bake for a further 3 hours. Remove the string and allow to cool. Apply 5 coats of satin varnish, allowing the varnish to dry between each coat.

4. Wrap sticky tape around the ends of the cord to prevent fraying. Lace the cord through the holes, threading on a tassel at the top of each corner. Cut off the tassels' hanging loops and adjust the tassels to hang between the holes. Fasten the cord ends together inside the box.

~ Bowls, Platters & Containers ~

71

Mexican Box

Chilli peppers, cacti, and sombreros are very popular South American themes, and with the rich, vibrant colour scheme on this practical box they suggest the *scenario of a bustling Mexican kitchen. The box is made complete with a small hole for a hook, so that it can be hung up in a handy position.*

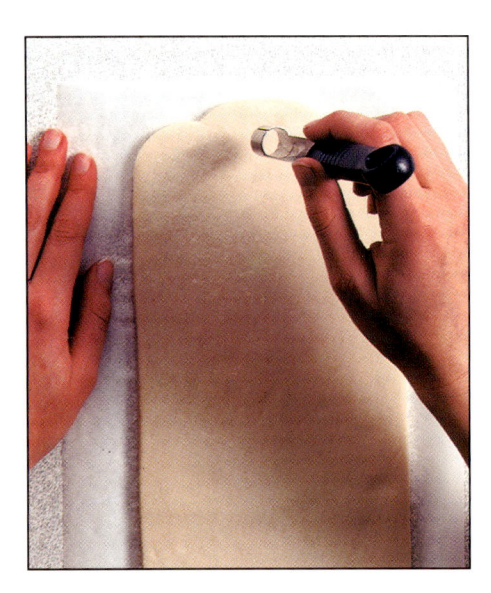

YOU WILL NEED
~

tracing paper and pencil

scissors

5 x quantity salt dough (see page 16) – you will find this easier to make in batches

rolling pin

baking parchment (parchment paper)

small, sharp knife

fruit corer

baking tray

non-stick tart baking tray (muffin pan)

dressmaking pin

fine-grade sandpaper

books or weights

string

acrylic gesso or matt emulsion (flat latex) paint

paintbrushes

acrylic or craft paints

polyurethane satin varnish

coloured raffia

all-purpose household glue

1. Scale the templates of the box back, side and front on page 152 to the size required and transfer to tracing paper. Cut out the shapes using scissors. Roll the dough out flat on baking parchment (parchment paper) to a thickness of 3/8 in (1 cm). Use the templates to cut 1 box back, 2 sides and 1 front. Also cut a square of 4¾ x 4¾ in (12 x 12 cm) for the base. Punch a hole in the top centre of the back panel with a fruit corer. Transfer the pieces to a baking tray and bake at 250°F/120°C/Gas ½ for 1 hour.

2. To make a sombrero, roll 2 balls of dough, each approximately 1¼ in (3 cm) in diameter. Flatten one ball for the brim and press into the cup of a non-stick tart baking tray (muffin pan), and mould the other ball into an oval for the crown. Flatten one end of this ball against the work surface, and gently squeeze the opposite end to narrow it into a blunt point. Moisten the centre of the sombrero and place the crown on top. Repeat to make 2 more sombreros, then bake in the oven at 250°F/120°C/Gas ½ for 2¼ hours.

~ Bowls, Platters & Containers ~

3. Roll 3 balls of dough ⅝ in (1.5 cm) in diameter and 1 ball ⅜ in (1 cm) in diameter. Mould into egg shapes, then flatten. Moisten and press the pieces together, forming a cactus shape. Roll 3 tiny balls of dough for flowers. Press to the cactus and indent with the head of a pin. Prick the cactus to suggest needles. Repeat to make 6 more cacti. ▸

~ *Mexican Box* ~

When baked, salt dough is strong enough to be hung on the wall as a container. If you are using it in the kitchen or bathroom, hang away from direct sources of steam as these may cause the dough to crumble slightly over time.

~ Bowls, Platters & Containers ~

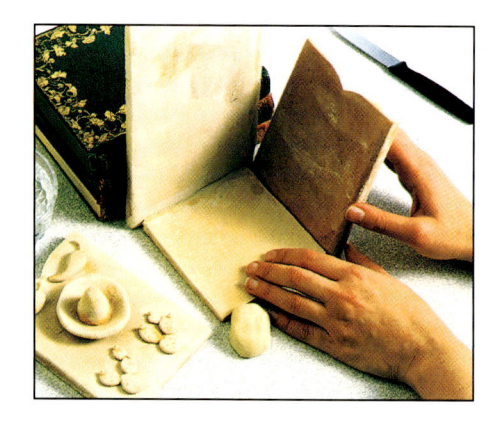

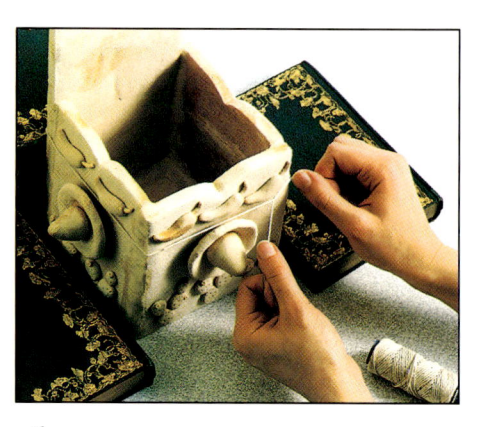

4. Roll a ¾ in (2 cm) diameter ball of dough for a chilli pepper. Roll into a sausage, squeeze one end and bend it upwards, then flatten the shape slightly. Roll a thin sausage to form a stalk, moisten one end and press it against the chilli. Bend the stalk into a curve. Repeat to make 8 more chilli peppers, all except one bent in the same direction. Bake the cacti and chillies in the oven at 250°F/120°C/Gas ½ for 25 minutes until slightly hardened.

5. Moisten the undersides of the sombreros, cacti and chillies, and smear with dough. Moisten the box front and side panels, and the top of the back panel. Gently press the sombreros, cacti and chillies into place. Return to the oven, with the box base, for 18 hours. Allow to cool, then sand the edges. Moisten the edges of the base and smear them with dough.

Moisten the lower edge and long edges of the back panel, and press it centrally upright against the base. Support the panel with books or weights. Moisten one long edge and the lower edge of a side panel and smear with dough. Position upright against the back panel and base. Support in place. Join the second side panel in the same way.

Moisten the back of the front panel around the straight edges and press in place to complete the box.

6. Tie string around the box to hold all the panels in place, and return it to the oven for 3 hours. Remove the string and allow to cool, then sand along the joins. Undercoat the box with acrylic gesso or matt emulsion (flat latex) paint, allow to dry and then paint with acrylic or craft paints. Apply 5 coats of satin varnish, allowing the varnish to dry between each coat. Tie a piece of raffia around each sombrero, and secure with a dab of glue.

~ *Mexican Chickens* ~

Salt dough is a common modelling and craft medium in South and Latin America. These small chickens are made entirely from salt dough, and are painted and made into festive decorations. Similar pieces are made into brooches with the addition of a pin-clasp glued on the back.

~ *Bowls, Platters & Containers* ~

Valentine's Boxes

Send your sweetheart a special gift in one of these precious lidded boxes, or simply use them to store your own knick-knacks. Any type of ovenproof dish can be used as a mould – even a very rounded one – as the dish can always stand securely on its little oval "feet".

YOU WILL NEED
(to make the heart-lidded bowl)

~

ovenproof dish

vegetable fat or cooking oil

1 quantity salt dough (see page 16)

rolling pin

chopping board and flour for dusting (optional)

baking parchment (parchment paper)

small, sharp knife

baking tray

pencil, paper and scissors or biscuit (cookie) cutter

acrylic gesso or matt emulsion (flat latex) paint

paintbrushes

acrylic or craft paints

polyurethane satin varnish

1. Turn over the ovenproof dish and smear the upturned side with vegetable fat or cooking oil. Roll the dough out flat on a lightly floured chopping board or baking parchment (parchment paper) to an approximate thickness of 3/8 in (1 cm). Carefully lift the dough and mould it on to the dish, cutting away the excess dough around the edge. Smooth the dough with a finger moistened in cold water.

2. Roll 4 balls of dough, each with an approximate diameter of about 5/8 in (1.5 cm). Moisten them with a little water and press gently on to the base of the bowl as "feet". Transfer the bowl, still on the ovenproof dish, on baking parchment (parchment paper), to a baking tray, and bake at 250°F/120°C/Gas ½ for 9 hours until hardened on top. ▶

~ Bowls, Platters & Containers ~

3. To make the lid, re-roll the remaining dough to an approximate thickness of 3/8 in (1 cm). From this, cut out a circular shape for the lid, using your own template or a biscuit (cookie) cutter, and cut out a heart for the handle. Transfer the pieces to a baking tray and bake for 45 minutes until hardened slightly.

4. Allow the pieces to cool and then attach the heart upright to the lid using wet dough, smoothing down the joins with a moistened finger. Place the lid back in the oven for 9 hours.

5. Remove the bowl and the lid from the oven and leave to cool, then carefully remove the ovenproof bowl from the dough. Paint an undercoat of acrylic gesso or matt emulsion (flat latex) paint on the bowl and the lid and leave to dry. Paint on your own colours and designs with acrylic or craft paints and leave to dry. Apply 5 coats of satin varnish to the inside and outside of the bowl and lid, allowing the varnish to dry between each coat.

~ *Valentine's Pots* ~

Customizing salt dough boxes (left and right) as gifts for friends and family is always enjoyable. Take advantage of the ridges formed by cutters to add extra coloured decoration, such as stripes and dots in contrasting colours. Motifs added on the lids provide both a handle and a decorative theme.

~ *Bowls, Platters & Containers* ~

~ Bowls, Platters & Containers ~

Needlework Casket

A lidded bowl provides a practical container for all sorts of small objects which otherwise tend to go astray. The delicately painted flowers on this

needlework casket resemble pretty embroidery motifs – you can either follow this design exactly, or paint on the flowers of your choice.

YOU WILL NEED

~

3 x quantity salt dough (see page 16)

rolling pin

baking parchment (parchment paper)

ovenproof bowl

cooking fat or vegetable oil

small, sharp knife

pair of compasses and pencil

thin card (cardboard)

scissors

masking tape

skewer

baking tray

acrylic gesso or matt emulsion (flat latex) paint

paintbrushes

acrylic or craft paints

polyurethane satin varnish

thick wire

small gold bead

large ceramic bead

~ ***Needlework Casket*** ~

A striking conical tidy, decorated both inside and out in a floral theme (far right).

1. Roll the dough out flat on baking parchment (parchment paper) to a thickness of 3/8 in (1 cm). Smear an upturned bowl with cooking fat or vegetable oil and carefully place the rolled-out dough over the bowl. Smooth it down and cut the edges level with a knife, then set on one side. To make a conical mould for the lid, draw a circle on thin card (cardboard) using a pair of compasses. As a guide, a 9½ in (24.5 cm) diameter circle was drawn for this 7 in (18 cm) bowl. Cut out the circle, then cut out a slice to the centre so that it is not too bulky.

2. Hold the circle over the bowl and overlap the straight edges to form a cone shape the same circumference as the open edges of the bowl so that it sits comfortably on top. Stick together the overlapping edges with masking tape. Smear the cone with cooking fat or vegetable oil. Roll the remaining dough out flat on baking parchment (parchment paper) to an approximate thickness of 3/8 in (1 cm), and carefully place it over the card (cardboard) cone.

~ *Bowls, Platters & Containers* ~

3. Cut away the excess dough, pat along the cut edge with a moistened finger to round it. Pierce a hole in the point of the cone with a skewer. Transfer the lid, on the parchment, to a baking tray, and bake it and the bowl in the oven at 250°F/120°C/Gas ½ for 7 hours. Remove the card (cardboard) from the lid and the bowl mould from the bowl, and bake for a further 2 hours. Allow to cool.

4. Undercoat the bowl and lid with acrylic gesso or matt emulsion (flat latex) paint. Leave to dry, then paint a background colour on the outside with acrylic or craft paints. Use a fine paintbrush to paint the flowers, referring to the picture as a guide, or paint your own floral design. Paint the inside of the bowl and lid in a contrasting colour, adding simple motifs at random.

5. Apply 5 coats of satin varnish, allowing the varnish to dry between each coat. Thread a small gold bead on to a 6 in (15 cm) length of wire, bend the wire ends downwards like a hairpin and thread on a large bead. Insert the wire ends into the hole in the point of the lid and splay the wire open inside the lid to hold the beads in place so that they can act as a handle.

~ *Bowls, Platters & Containers* ~

Flower Vase

This vibrant bottomless vase with its star-shaped rim is designed to be placed over a jar of water which can then be filled with your favourite flowers. Take care when filling the jar not to splash water on the vase, as this may damage the dough and cause it to crumble.

YOU WILL NEED
~

1 quantity salt dough (see page 16)

rolling pin

chopping board and flour for dusting

baking parchment (parchment paper)

large cardboard tube (e.g., postage tube), approximately 12 in (30 cm) long

baking tray

small, sharp knife

acrylic gesso or matt emulsion (flat latex) paint

paintbrushes

acrylic or craft paints

polyurethane satin varnish

~ *Flower Vase* ~

This bottomless vase can be made in a variety of sizes depending on the containers to be used inside. Choose bright, cheerful colours for the tartan-style striped design, and match them with the bouquets of flowers for a co-ordinating look (far right).

1. Roll the dough out flat on a lightly floured chopping board or baking parchment (parchment paper) to a thickness of ⅝ in (1.5 cm). Use the dough to cover one half of the tube, including the inside. Transfer the tube, on baking parchment (parchment paper), to a baking tray, and bake in the oven at 250°F/120°C/Gas ½ for approximately 1 hour.

2. Cover the remaining part of the tube with dough, smoothing down the joins with a moistened finger. Return the tube to the oven for another hour.

Re-roll the remaining dough to an approximate thickness of ⅜ in (1 cm) and cut out 8 triangles. Transfer the triangles, on parchment, to a baking tray, and bake for 3 hours, until they are hard.

~ Bowls, Platters & Containers ~

3. When the pieces are cool, smear salt dough around the rim of the vase and stick on the triangles, using a little water to help them stick. Smooth down any visible joins with a moistened finger. Place the vase back in the oven, standing it upright, for a further 12 hours.

4. When the vase is cool, paint on an undercoat of acrylic gesso or matt emulsion (flat latex) paint and leave to dry. Decorate the vase with an assortment of coloured paints and leave to dry. Apply 5 coats of satin varnish, allowing the varnish to dry between each coat.

~ Bowls, Platters & Containers ~

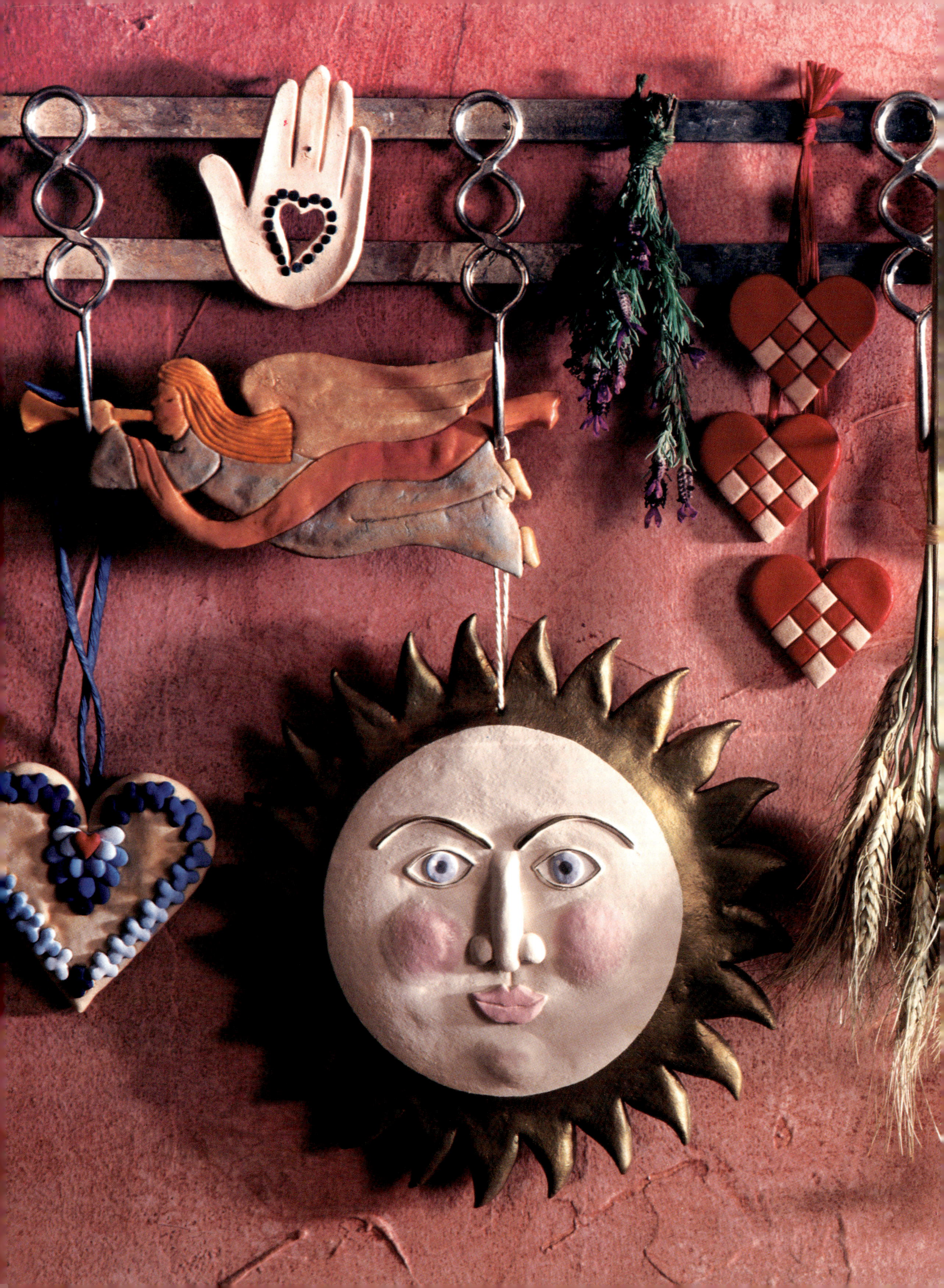

Wall Ornaments

The traditional applications of salt dough are particularly well suited to the modelling of flat, two-dimensional objects. It is an ideal medium for producing practical ornaments of this kind as the baking process strengthens the sculpture and allows the fixing of a hanging hook or ring. Different decorative techniques can be used to colour or give texture to the relatively flat plane. Traditional folk art themes such as hearts and hands make perfect two-dimensional wall ornaments, and can be adapted to practical uses too, in keyracks or clocks, for example.

~ *Perfect Plaques* ~

From the heavenly to the pagan, these salt dough wall decorations present an extraordinary number of guises. Folk art marries with ancient sun symbolism, and Scandinavian influences with traditional country styles in a wonderfully eclectic range.

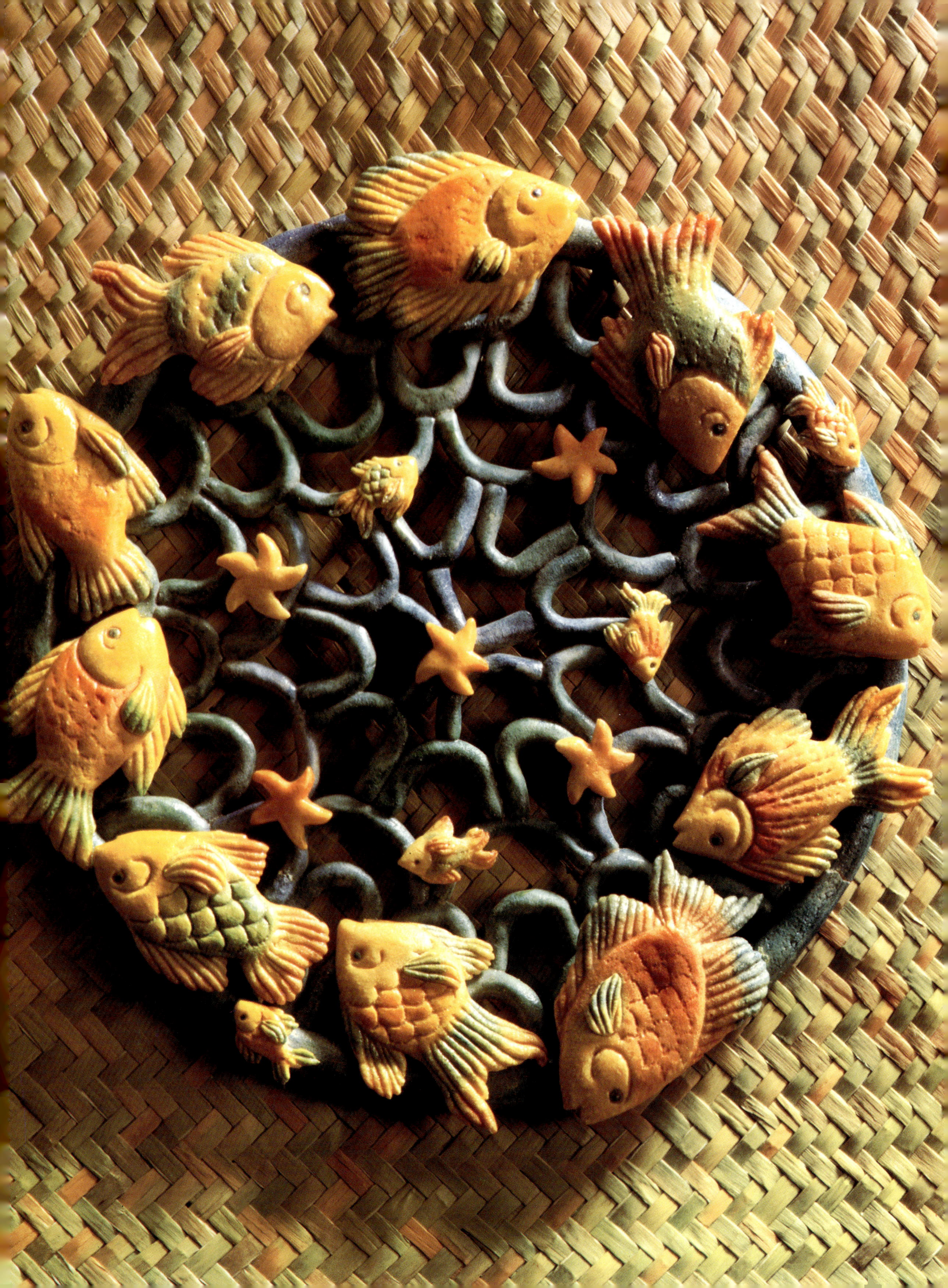

Fish Plaque

Create a stunning decoration for a wall or even a table centrepiece with this circular plaque. The large fish are traced from a template and so are very easy to make, and the plaque is painted with blended watercolour paints to achieve the natural, varied effect.

YOU WILL NEED

~

plate, approximately 8½ in (22 cm) in diameter
pencil
baking parchment (parchment paper)
1 quantity salt dough (see page 16)
small, sharp knife
tracing paper
scissors
rolling pin
thick needle
baking tray
watercolour paints
paintbrushes
ceramic tile or old plate
polyurethane satin varnish

~ *Fish Plaque* ~

This top-to-tail fish sequence with small details in the centre portions of the plaque is an example of the strength of salt dough once baked. It is best mounted as a wall decoration, or perhaps as part of a collection of several similar plaques on a dresser shelf.

1. Using a pencil, draw around an upturned plate on to baking parchment (parchment paper) to use as a guide for the plaque size. Roll sausages of dough ⅝ in (1.5 cm) thick and lay them along the circumference of the drawn circle until they meet. The sausages can be joined using either a finger moistened in cold water, or a small piece of dough, as the joins will be hidden by the fish when they are placed around the edge.

2. Roll sausages of dough to a thickness of ¼ in (5 mm), and cut them into about 20 pieces, each 2¼ in (5.5 cm) long. Moisten the ends and bend the pieces into semi-circles. Press the ends to the plaque rim, placing the semi-circles side by side. Work the next row in the same way, cutting the sausages into 1¾ in (4.5 cm) lengths. Continue filling in the circle, cutting sausages for the third row into 2¼ in (5.5 cm) lengths and butting their ends against alternate semi-circles in the second row. The sausages in the fourth row should be 1¾ in (4.5 cm) long, and the three centre sausages 1¼ in (3 cm) long. ▶

~ Wall Ornaments ~

3. Size the templates on page 153, transfer to tracing paper, and draw some fish of your own design the same size too, if you wish. Cut out the shapes. Roll the dough out flat on baking parchment (parchment paper) to a thickness of 1/4 in (5 mm), and use the templates to cut out 10 fish. Cut out 5 smaller fish and 5 starfish freehand. Pat the cut edges with a moistened finger to round them. Use a thick needle to mark eyes, scales, patterns and other details on the fish, by either pricking the designs or drawing them with the needle.

4. Mould fins from dough, moisten them and press to the fish. Indent the fins and tails with the needle. Transfer all the pieces, on the parchment, to a baking tray and bake in the oven at 250°F/120°C/Gas 1/2 for 1 hour. Allow to cool, then moisten the undersides of the fish and starfish. Smear with dough and press to the plaque. Bake for a further 10 hours. When cool, paint the plaque with watercolour paints, mixing the colours on a ceramic tile or an old plate. Apply 5 coats of satin varnish, allowing the varnish to dry between each coat.

~ *By the Seashore* ~

Seaside objects such as shells and starfish in different shapes and sizes, make excellent templates and moulds. If left unpainted, the salt dough shapes seem sun-bleached and surprisingly realistic, retaining minutely detailed indentations (right). Alternatively, watercolours can be used to decorate the dough models, creating subtle shades of contrasting colours (left).

~ *Wall Ornaments* ~

86

~ *Wall Ornaments* ~

Folk Angel

A heralding angel is a familiar symbol of American folk art. This charming example, perhaps hung from a fine ribbon, would make a delightful housewarming gift.

The angel is created from a single piece of dough, simply but effectively decorated using a series of indented lines to pick out the details and then painted in clear colours.

YOU WILL NEED
~

1 quantity salt dough (see page 16)

rolling pin

baking parchment (parchment paper)

tracing paper and pencil

scissors

small, sharp knife

dressmaking pin

wire paperclip

wire-cutters

baking tray

watercolour paints

paintbrushes

polyurethane matt varnish

coloured string or fine ribbon

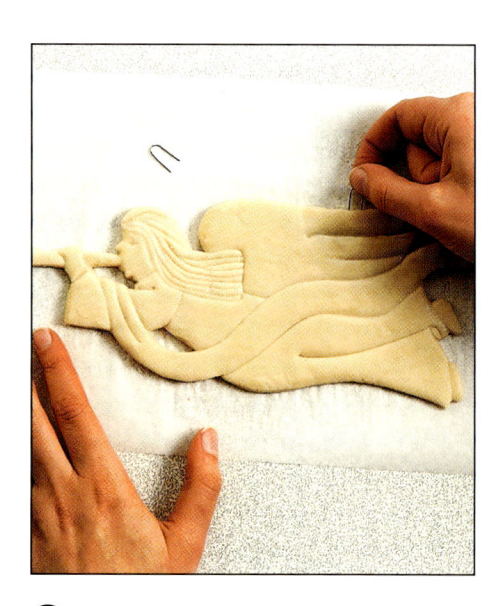

1. Roll the dough out flat on baking parchment (parchment paper) to a thickness of ³/₈ in (1 cm). Size the angel template on page 153, transfer on to tracing paper and cut it out. Place on the dough and cut out the shape with a sharp knife. Remove the template and pat the cut edges with a moistened finger to neaten them. Replace the template and transfer the design details by pricking along the lines with a pin, working on one line at a time. Lightly moisten the pricked line, then draw along it with the tip of the knife, leaning the blade towards you then away from you to make an inverted division.

2. Prick and indent all the lines in this way. Use wire-cutters to cut a wire paperclip in half. Insert the 2 outer halves into the cut edges at the positions of the crosses, leaving the loops just visible. These will be used to hang up the angel – the baking process fixes them in the model very firmly. Transfer the angel, on the parchment, to a baking tray, and bake in the oven at 250°F/120°C/Gas ½ for 10 hours. Allow to cool.

~ *Wall Ornaments* ~

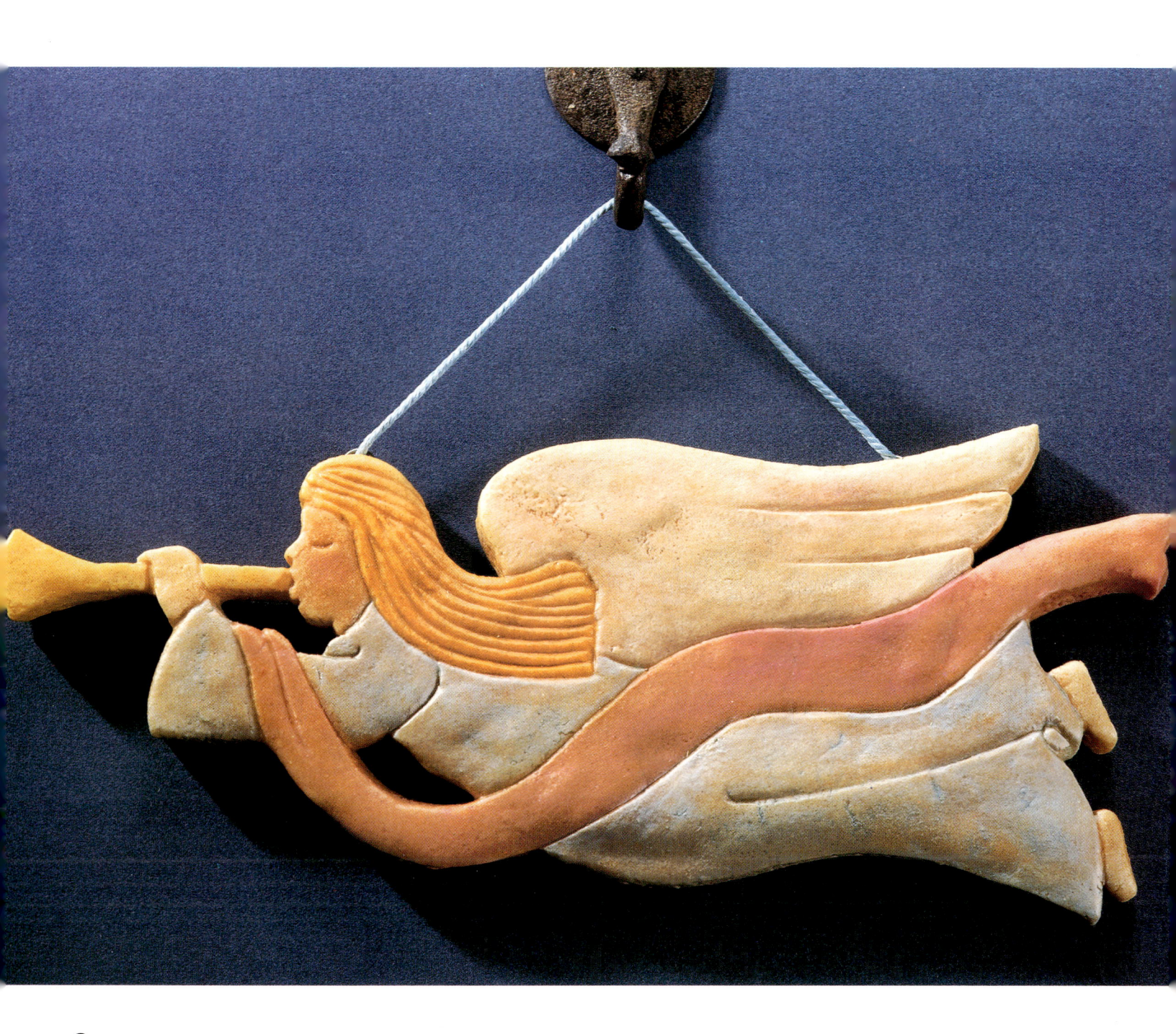

3. Paint the model with watercolour paints, mixing the colours with white to lighten them and applying the paint thinly so that the dough shows through. Leave the flesh areas unpainted, but highlight the cheek with a little pink. When the paint has dried, apply 5 coats of varnish. Hang the angel on coloured string or fine ribbon. ▶

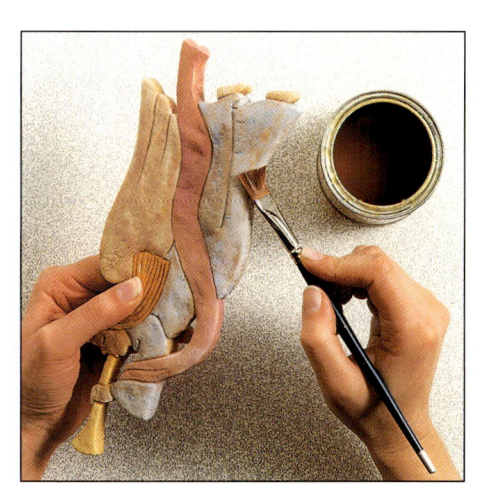

~ Folk Angel ~

This plaque-style angel is a perfect model to create from salt dough. When using flat pieces of dough, the baking process takes place evenly throughout the sheet of dough, so avoiding any hardening inconsistencies. Any indented decorative detail shows up especially clearly on a flat surface.

~ Wall Ornaments ~

~ Shooting Stars ~

Celestial, magical shooting stars formed from salt dough using antique mousse moulds (left and right).

~ Cherubic Head ~

Other angelic figures can be made from salt dough, and displayed in the home or conservatory. The inspiration for this wonderful winged cherub comes from a stone carving on an old English gravestone (below).

~ Wall Ornaments ~

Lion's Head

The stone-like appearance of this regal lion's head is achieved by using double the quantity of the salt in the salt-dough recipe. Blended watercolour paints and a sparing application of a wax metallic finish also help to create the very effective rough surface texture.

YOU WILL NEED

~

baking foil

baking parchment
(parchment paper)

1 quantity salt dough
(see page 16), made with 1 cup
extra salt

pencil

small, sharp knife

baking tray

wire paperclip

wire-cutters

watercolour paints

paintbrushes

ceramic tile or old plate

wax metallic finish

polyurethane matt varnish

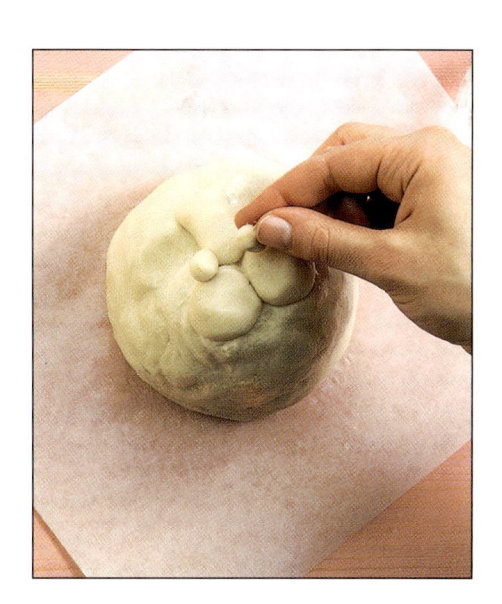

1. Scrunch a piece of baking foil into a 4¼ in (10.5 cm) diameter ball. Mould the ball into a fat pear shape and press it on to baking parchment (parchment paper), placing the narrow end – which will be the tip of the nose – facing upwards. Form thin pieces of dough between your fingers and press the pieces on to the foil mould. Smooth over the dough with a moistened finger. Gently depress the dough on either side of the centre with your thumbs to form the eye sockets.

2. Roll a sausage 2¼ in (5.5 cm) long and ⅝ in (1.5 cm) thick for the nose. Moisten it, then flatten and press between the eye sockets. Roll 2 balls of dough, each 1 in (2.5 cm) in diameter, for the muzzle. Press underneath to the nose. Roll 2 balls of dough ⅜ in (1 cm) in diameter for nostrils, and press on either side of the nose. Smooth all the pieces on to the head with a moistened finger, and indent the nostrils with a pencil point. ▶

~ Wall Ornaments ~

~ *Lion's Head* ~

All sorts of stone carvings can provide inspiration for salt dough modelling. Gargoyles, church carvings, old beams, inset plaques, pillars, columns, and gravestones all feature decorative and often unusual figures. This Lion's Head (right) is very similar to medieval chivalric gargoyles.

3. Roll a thin sausage of dough as a lower lip. Press it under the muzzle and smooth on to the head. Indent the mouth with the knife tip, laying the blade against the muzzle to round off the surface.

4. Roll a long sausage of dough for the eyebrows, and 2 balls of dough, each ¾ in (2 cm) in diameter, for the cheeks. Flatten the balls and press the pieces to the head, then smooth with a moistened finger.

5. Draw the eyes with the knife tip and moisten the outlines. Roll thin sausages of dough and lay them along the outlines. Flatten 2 small balls of dough for eyeballs, moisten them and press in place. Indent the eyeballs with the pencil point. Roll 11 balls of dough, each 1½ in (3.5 cm) in diameter, for the mane.

Flatten the balls slightly and pull out one side of each to form triangles. Press around the head.

6. Pull out the tips of the triangles and coil them to one side. Indent curling divisions with the knife tip. Transfer the model, on the parchment, to a baking tray, and bake in the oven at 250°F/120°C/Gas ½ for 6 hours, until the top has hardened. Allow to cool. Snip a wire paperclip in half with wire-cutters. Smear dough on to the back of the model and insert the outer halves of the paperclip at each side.

7. Return the model to the oven for a further 6 hours, then allow to cool. Mix white watercolour paint with a little cadmium orange on a ceramic tile or old plate and use to paint the model. Emphasize some areas with a darker blend of the colours. When the paint has dried, rub a wax metallic finish sparingly into the surface. Apply 5 coats of matt varnish, allowing the varnish to dry between each coat.

~ *Wall Ornaments* ~

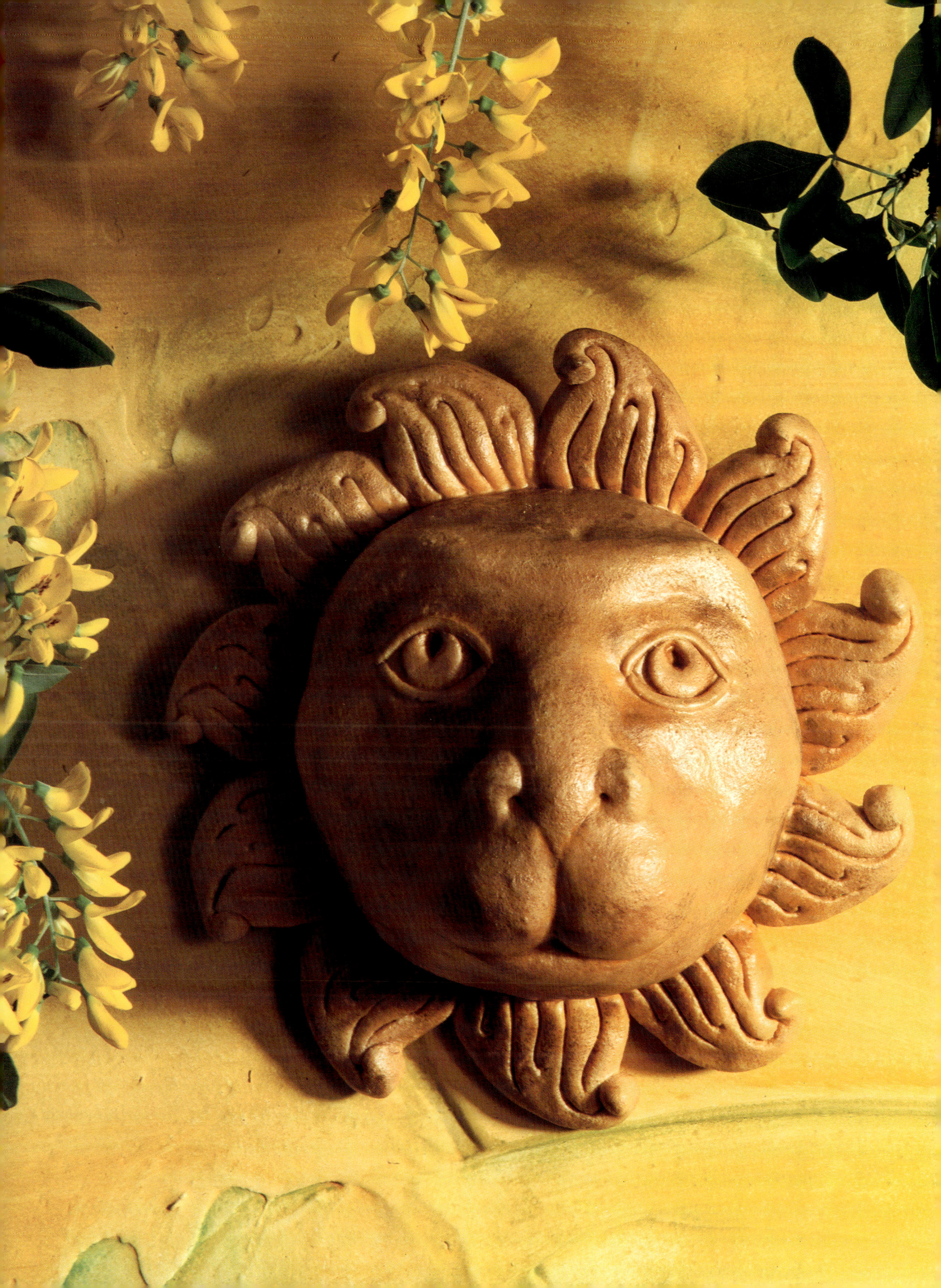

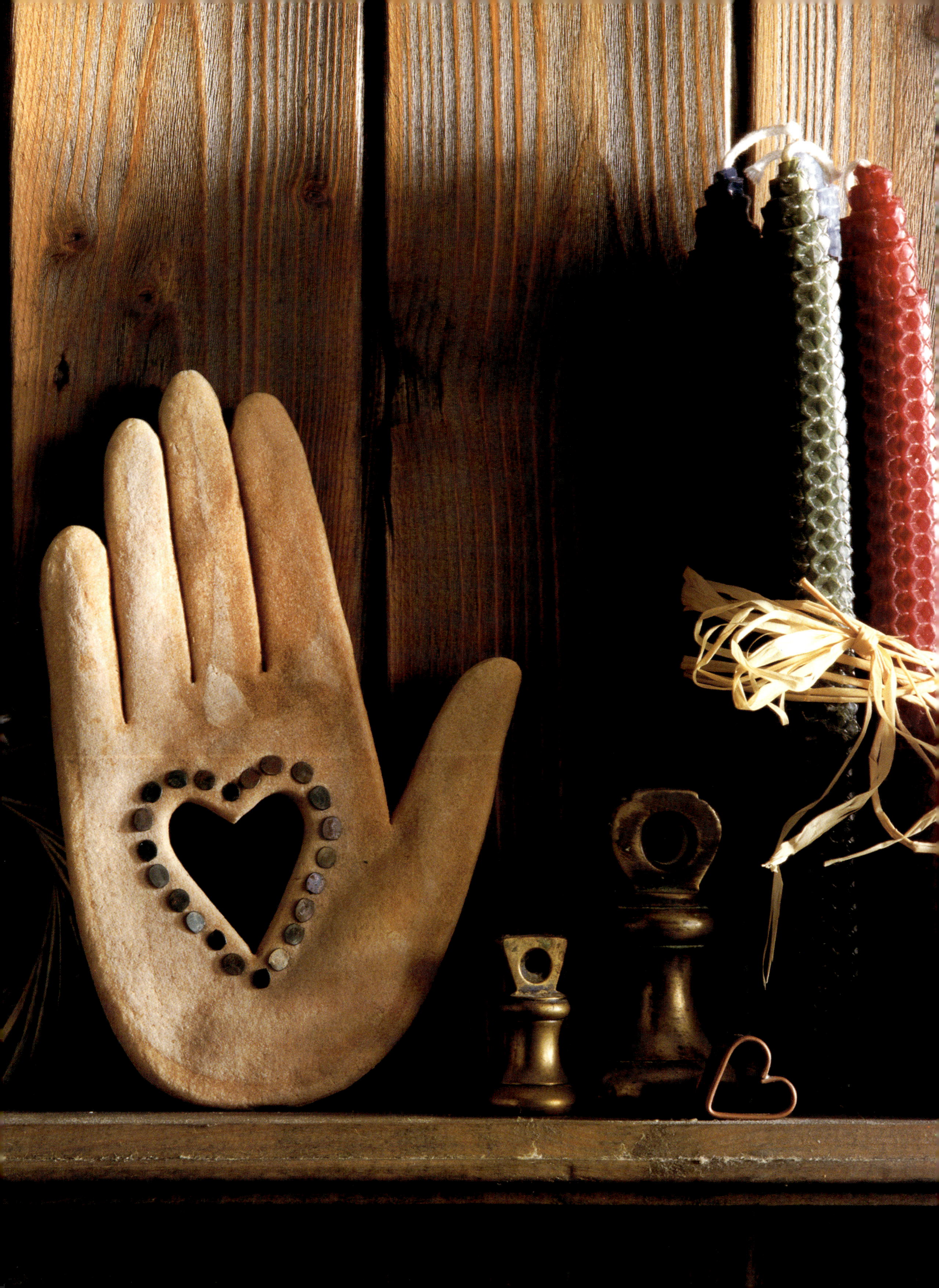

Shaker Hand

Make a special record of your friends and family by drawing around their hands and preserving them in salt dough. *This motif is typical of the traditional Shaker style found in many North American homes.*

1. Roll the dough out on baking parchment (parchment paper) to a thickness of ⅝ in (1.5 cm). Lay your hand flat on to the dough with your fingers together. Use a knitting needle to trace around the edge and mark the fingers, then cut out the hand outline using a sharp knife. Pat the cut edges with a moistened finger to round them.

YOU WILL NEED
(to make 1 hand)

~

½ *quantity salt dough*
(see page 16)

rolling pin

baking parchment
(parchment paper)

knitting needle

small, sharp knife

heart-shaped cutter (optional)

eyelet loop

modelling tool

tin-tacks

baking tray

polyurethane matt varnish

2. Cut out a heart shape from the palm, either cutting freehand with a small knife, or using a heart shaped pastry cutter. Turn the hand over and insert an eyelet loop for hanging it up. The loop will bake in hard and form a secure hanger. ▶

~ *Shaker Hand* ~

The unpainted salt dough of this hand makes it appear startlingly lifelike. The motif of a bordered heart is reminiscent of North American styles of the 1800s, often found in punched metal designs.

~ *Wall Ornaments* ~

3. Use a modelling tool or tip of the knife to mark the fingers. Press tin-tacks into the dough to outline the cut-out heart. Repeat the process to make as many hands as you wish. Transfer the hands, on baking parchment (parchment paper) to a baking tray, and bake at 250°F/ 120°C/Gas ½ for 9 hours. Allow to cool, then apply 5 coats of matt varnish, allowing the varnish to dry between each coat.

~ *Hands Galore* ~

These miniature models (right) are produced from a template taken from a child's hand, while the clasped hands theme (below) takes its inspiration from a carving in an old graveyard.

~ *Wall Ornaments* ~

~ *Wall Ornaments* ~

97

~ *Indian Hand* ~

This elaborately decorated salt dough hand takes its inspiration from festive henna hand stencils. The stencil was applied to the raw dough and created a very fine patterned texture across the surface (above).

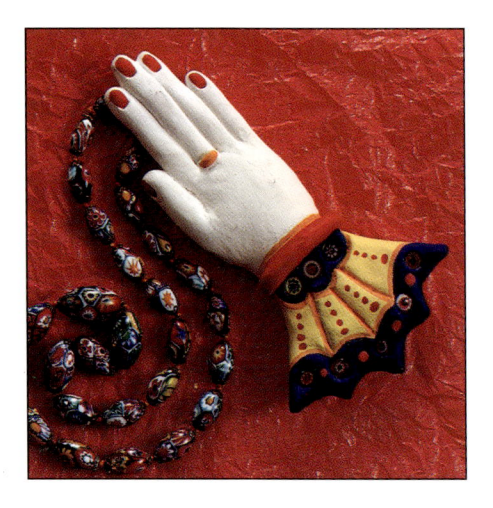

~ *Mexican Hand* ~

This hand is studded with pretty Florentine glass beads which are embedded in the decorative frilled cuff. The coloured beads withstand the heat of the oven well and become firmly fixed in place during the baking process.

~ *Wall Ornaments* ~

Sponged Goose Keyrack

This colourful keyrack makes an unusual wall decoration and is a practical place to keep those keys that always seem to go astray! The natural "feathered" effect on the goose is created by stippling and sponging on the colour in a slightly uneven way.

YOU WILL NEED
~

pencil and tracing paper
2 x quantity salt dough
(see page 16)
rolling pin
baking parchment
(parchment paper)
small, sharp knife
dressmaking pin
modelling tool (optional)
glass toy eye or black bead
4 small brass hooks
2 eyelet loops
baking tray
acrylic gesso or matt emulsion
(flat latex) paint
paintbrushes
acrylic or craft paints
natural sponge
polyurethane matt varnish
short length of wire

1. Size the goose template on page 153 and transfer to tracing paper. Roll the dough out on baking parchment (parchment paper) to a thickness of 3/8 in (1 cm). Carefully cut around the template using a sharp knife, and transfer all the markings by pricking with a pin. Pat the cut edges with a moistened finger to round and smooth them, then use a modelling tool or the tip of a knife to define the lines on the goose wings and body. Press the eye or black bead into place on the head.

2. Roll a 6 x 3/8 in (15 x 1 cm) sausage from the remaining dough, moisten it and attach to the lower edge of the model. Use a modelling tool or knife tip to mark the reeds. Push 4 hooks into this supporting roll, 1½ in (3.5 cm) apart, as marked on the template. Insert 2 eyelet loops into the reverse side of the model, using the marked crosses as a guide. Transfer the model, on the parchment, to a baking tray, and bake at 250°F/120°C/Gas ½ for 12 hours. Allow to cool. ▶

~ Wall Ornaments ~

3. Paint the whole model with a base coat of acrylic gesso or matt emulsion (flat latex) paint. When dry, apply stippled and sponged colour using a dry brush and a small natural sponge. Leave to dry, then apply 5 coats of matt varnish, allowing the varnish to dry between each coat. Fix a length of wire between the eyelets on the back and hang up.

~ *Dough Menagerie* ~

The Sponged Goose Keyrack is sturdy enough to hold several keys at a time (right). The same sponging paint effect can be used for all manner of animals. This collection (below) was made using animal-shaped pastry cutters and suspended from hand-woven silk ribbons.

~ Wall Ornaments ~

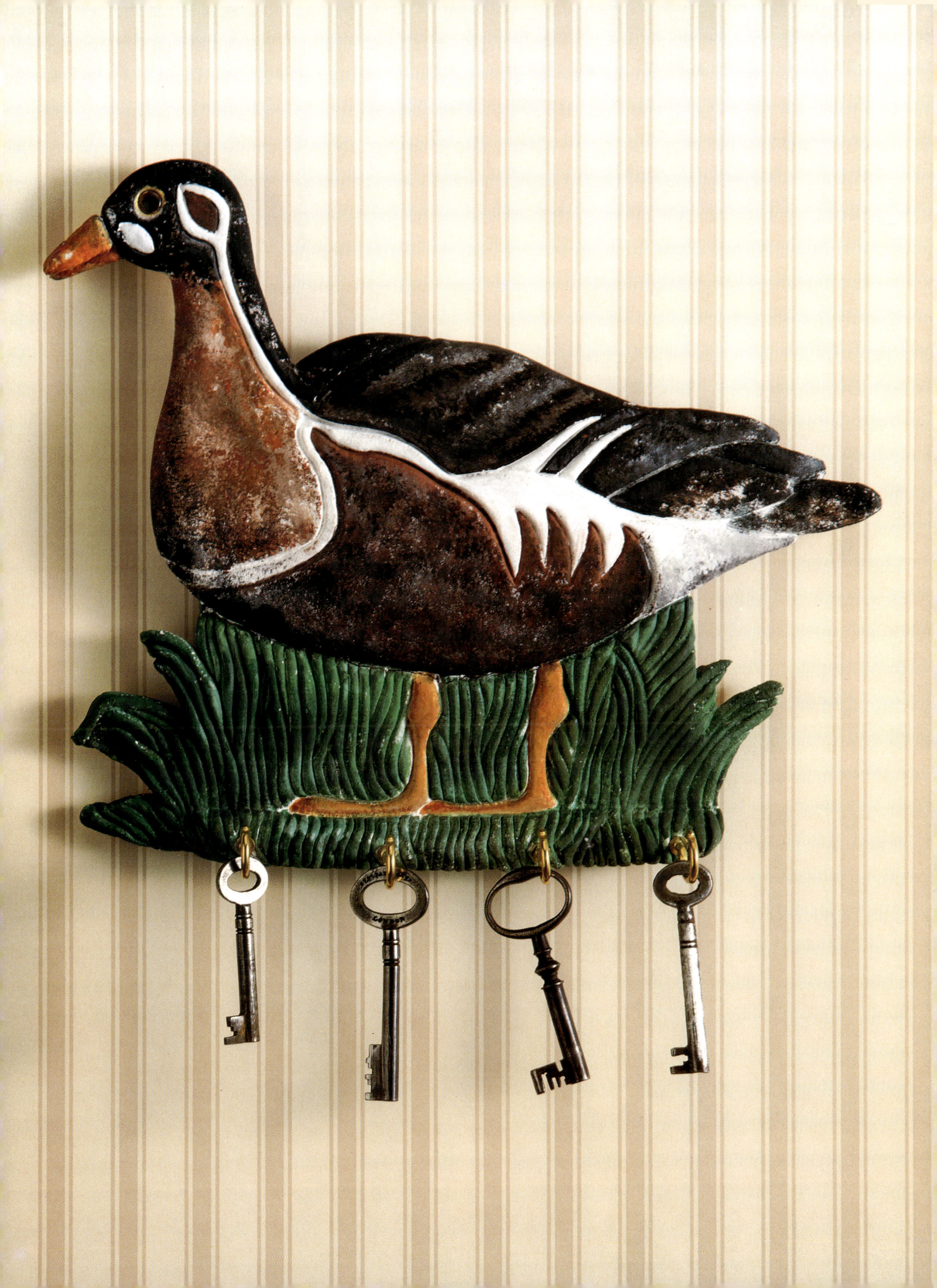

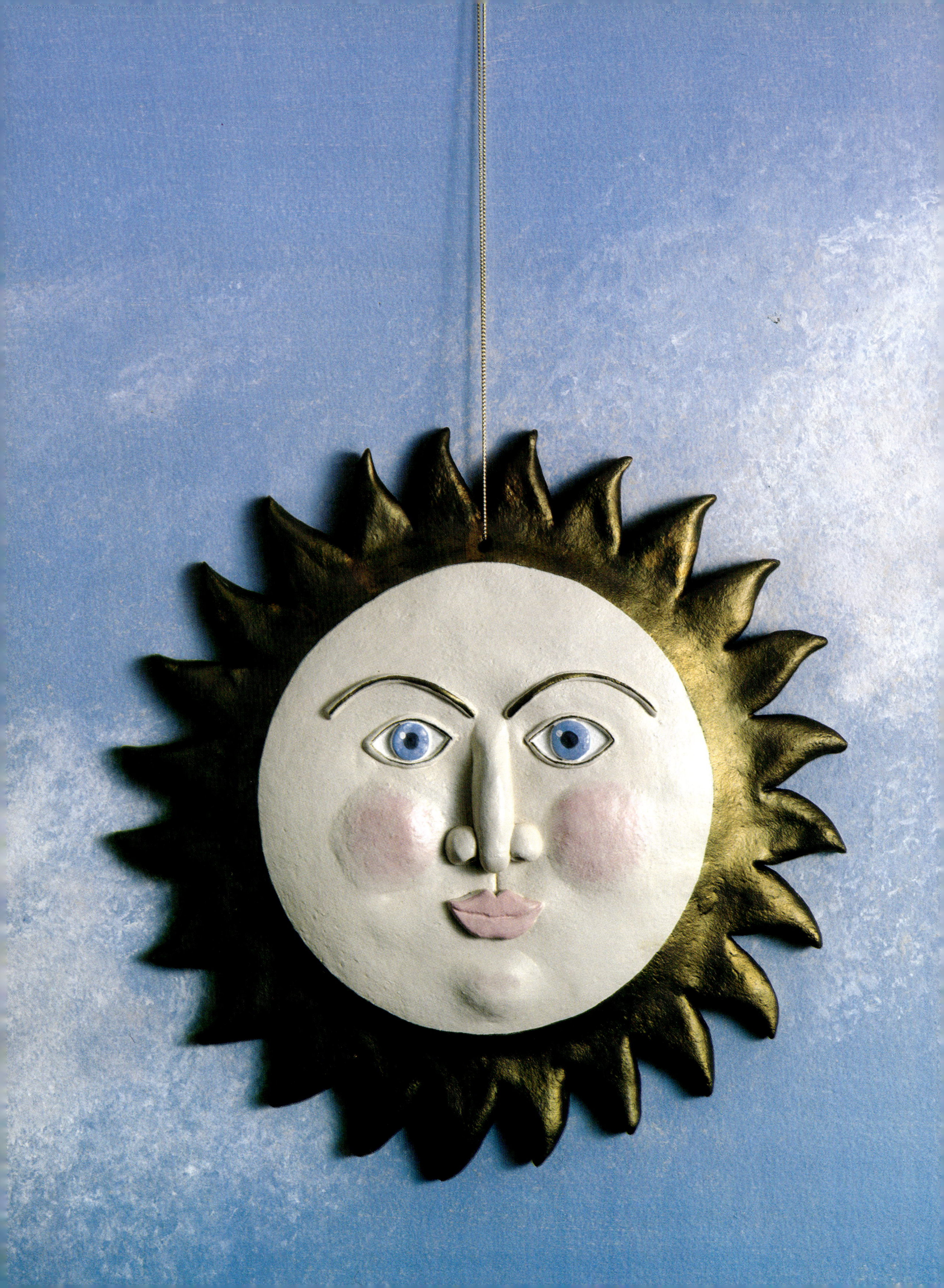

Sun Plaque

A pastel-coloured sun makes a welcoming decoration when hung on a wall. This example has a wonderfully expressive face, created by moulding pieces of dough separately and then smoothing them on to the base shape. The cheeks and chin colours are sponged.

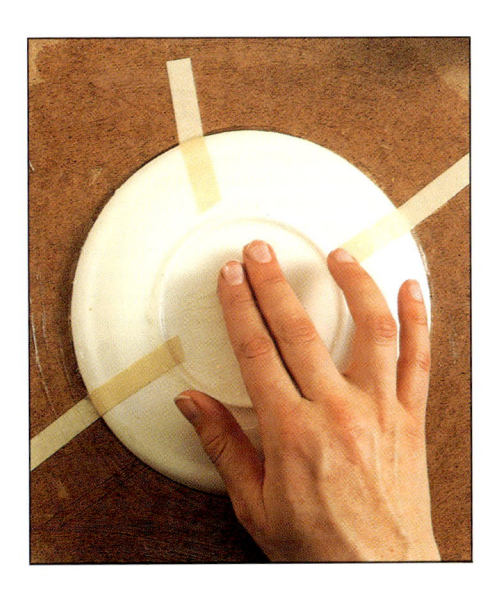

YOU WILL NEED

~

7 in (18 cm) diameter ovenproof plate

sheet of hardboard (to fit oven)

masking tape

cooking fat or vegetable oil

2 x quantity salt dough (see page 16)

rolling pin

tracing paper and pencil

scissors

small, sharp knife

skewer

acrylic gesso or matt emulsion (flat latex) paint

paintbrushes

acrylic or craft paints

ceramic tile

natural sponge

polyurethane satin varnish

fine gold cord

1. Position the plate upside-down on the centre of the sheet of hardboard, and secure with masking tape. Smear the plate and hardboard with cooking fat or vegetable oil – this will act as a releasing agent so that the plaque can be removed easily. Roll the dough out flat to a thickness of 3/8 in (1 cm). Carefully lift the rolled dough, supporting it underneath with your hand, and place it centrally over the plate.

2. Size the sun, eye and mouth templates on page 154 and transfer to tracing paper. Cut out the shapes and the inner circle of the sun from the remaining dough. Place the sun-ray template on the dough with the plate in the centre. Cut the dough around the outer edges using a sharp knife, remove the template and then pat the cut edges of the dough with a moistened finger to round and smooth them. ▶

~ *Sun Plaque* ~

This flat plaque has features added in relief formed from separate balls of dough moulded into shape.

~ Wall Ornaments ~

3. Roll a sausage of dough ½ in (1.25 cm) thick and 2¼ in (5.5 cm) long for the nose. Moisten the centre of the sun and position the nose. Stroke the top of the nose on to the face. Roll two ½ in (1.25 cm) diameter balls of dough for nostrils, and press on either side of the nose. Poke a pencil point into each nostril. Press the face to the left and right of the nose with your thumbs to make depressions for the eye sockets.

4. Place two eye templates in position on the dough, lightly draw around them with the tip of the knife, then remove the templates.

5. Roll thin sausages of dough and lay them along the eye lines. Next, roll two ⅜ in (1 cm) diameter balls of dough for eyeballs, flatten them and place on the eyes. Draw a line ⅝ in (1.5 cm) long down from the nose with the knife tip. Roll a small piece of dough out flat to a thickness of 5 mm (¼ in). Use the mouth template to cut a mouth from the dough. Draw the division of the lips with the knife tip. Press the mouth in place.

6. Roll two ¾ in (2 cm) diameter balls of dough for the cheeks and a ⅝ in (1.5 cm) ball for the chin. Flatten the balls, then press on to the face. Smooth outwards to blend to the face. Roll thin sausages for eyebrows. Pierce a hole at the top of the plaque with a skewer. Bake at 250°F/120°C/ Gas ½ for 12 hours, removing the plate and upturning the plaque when the top of the face is hard.

7. Undercoat the sun with acrylic gesso or matt emulsion (flat latex) paint. When dry, paint with acrylic or craft paints, adding a blush of colour by mixing pink and a pale flesh-coloured paint. Apply a thin film of the pink paint to a ceramic tile. Gently dab the paint on to the cheeks and chin with a natural sponge. When dry, apply 5 coats of satin varnish. Hang up the sun with gold cord.

~ *Wall Ornaments* ~

~ Sun & Moon ~

Verdigris and bronze paint effects are used to decorate this lively many-rayed sun (below). Again the features are built up in relief on a flat background while the rays are set at jagged angles to create the impression of movement. The silver crescent moon (right) is formed inside a copper mould (far right). A star is added to the silver cord for extra decoration.

~ Wall Ornaments ~

Tex-Mex Clock

Add a touch of the Wild West to your home with this cheerful "cowboy" wall clock. You can obtain the clock mechanism and hands from craft shops. If you prefer, you could make the clock circular, or even square, and arrange the motifs differently.

YOU WILL NEED
~

tracing paper and pencil

scissors

2 x quantity salt dough (see page 16)

rolling pin

baking parchment (parchment paper)

dressmaking pin

16 silver star studs

baking tray

paintbrushes

acrylic or craft paints

silver craft paint

polyurethane matt varnish

clock mechanism and hands

~ *Tex-Mex Clock* ~

This clever clock uses the cowboy desert theme to create the numerals out of "spur" stars, picking up the same motif on the boots (far right). Make some extra cacti and use as brooches or earrings.

1. Size the clock, cacti and cowboy-boot templates on page 156, transfer to tracing paper and cut out the shapes. Roll the dough out flat on baking parchment (parchment paper) to a thickness of 3/8 in (1 cm). Place the clock template on top and cut around the outer edge, using a sharp knife. Push a pin through the template into the clock at the dots to mark the positions of the hours and clock centre. Remove the template. Insert the star studs at the hour points and along the lower edge at the marked dots.

2. Cut a hole at the centre large enough for the clockwork spoke to be inserted through it, and add an extra 1/8 in (3 mm) to the diameter of the hole to allow for painting and varnishing. Roll the remaining dough out flat on baking parchment (parchment paper) to a thickness of 1/4 in (5 mm). Use the templates to cut 4 cacti and a pair of cowboy boots, cutting the boot straps and spurs separately. Pat the cut edges of the pieces with a moistened finger to round them. Indent the details with the tip of the knife.

~ *Wall Ornaments* ~

3. Moisten the cowboy boots and carefully place the boot straps and spurs in place. Emboss a "stud" on each spur with the head of a pin. Transfer all the pieces, on the parchment, to a baking tray, and bake in the oven at 250°F/120°C/Gas ½ for 1 hour. Moisten the undersides of the cacti and cowboy boots. Smear sparingly with dough and press in position on the clock. Return to the oven for a further 9 hours, then allow to cool.

Paint the clock with acrylic or craft paints, applying it fairly thinly to allow the dough to show through in places. Use a fine brush to paint the "stitching" on the boots, and paint the clock hands and details on the spurs with silver craft paint. Apply 5 coats of matt varnish. Assemble the clock mechanism and hands.

~ *Wall Ornaments* ~

"Gingerbread" Heart

Paper ribbon is now widely available from craft shops and larger stores, and adds the perfect finishing touch to this heart.

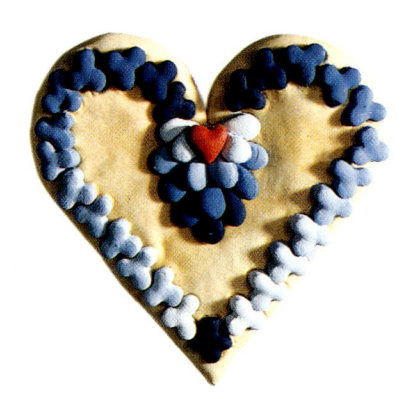

The small motifs are cut from the dough using aspic cutters, and are then attached to the main heart shape in a border pattern.

YOU WILL NEED
~

pencil and paper

scissors

1 quantity salt dough (see page 16)

rolling pin

baking parchment (parchment paper)

small, sharp knife

aspic cutters

metal eyelet loop

baking tray

acrylic gesso or matt emulsion (flat latex) paint

paintbrushes

acrylic or craft paints

polyurethane matt varnish

paper ribbon

~ *"Gingerbread" Hearts* ~

The designs of these Germanic hearts are based on edible gingerbread and fondant cakes. They are formed from a natural dough base with painted motifs applied on top. The paint shades are carefully chosen to produce contrasting and complementary patterns.

1. Size the larger heart template on page 154, transfer to paper and cut it out. Roll an orange-sized ball of dough out flat on baking parchment (parchment paper) to a thickness of ⅜ in (1 cm). Place the template on the dough and cut around the edge. Pat the raw edges to round them. Roll the remaining dough out to a thickness of ¼ in (5 mm) and cut out shapes with aspic cutters. Moisten the border of the main heart shape and apply the small shapes. Fix the eyelet loop to the top of the heart. Transfer the model, on the parchment, to a baking tray, and bake in the oven at 250°F/120°C/Gas ½ for 9 hours.

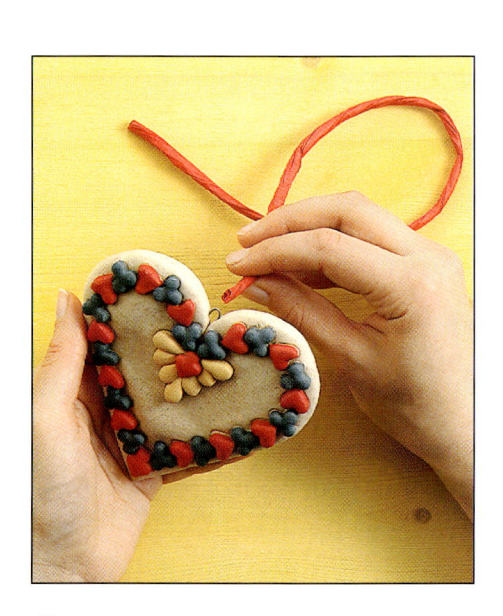

2. When the model is cool, paint on an undercoat of acrylic gesso or matt emulsion (flat latex) paint. Leave to dry, then pick out the applied decoration with bright acrylic or craft paints, using a fine paintbrush to avoid getting paint on the base heart. When dry, apply 5 coats of matt varnish, allowing the varnish to dry between each coat. Cut a 16 in (40 cm) length of paper ribbon, thread it through the eyelet and tie in a reef knot about 4 in (10 cm) from the heart. Unravel the ribbon and cut out a chevron shape from each end.

~ *Wall Ornaments* ~

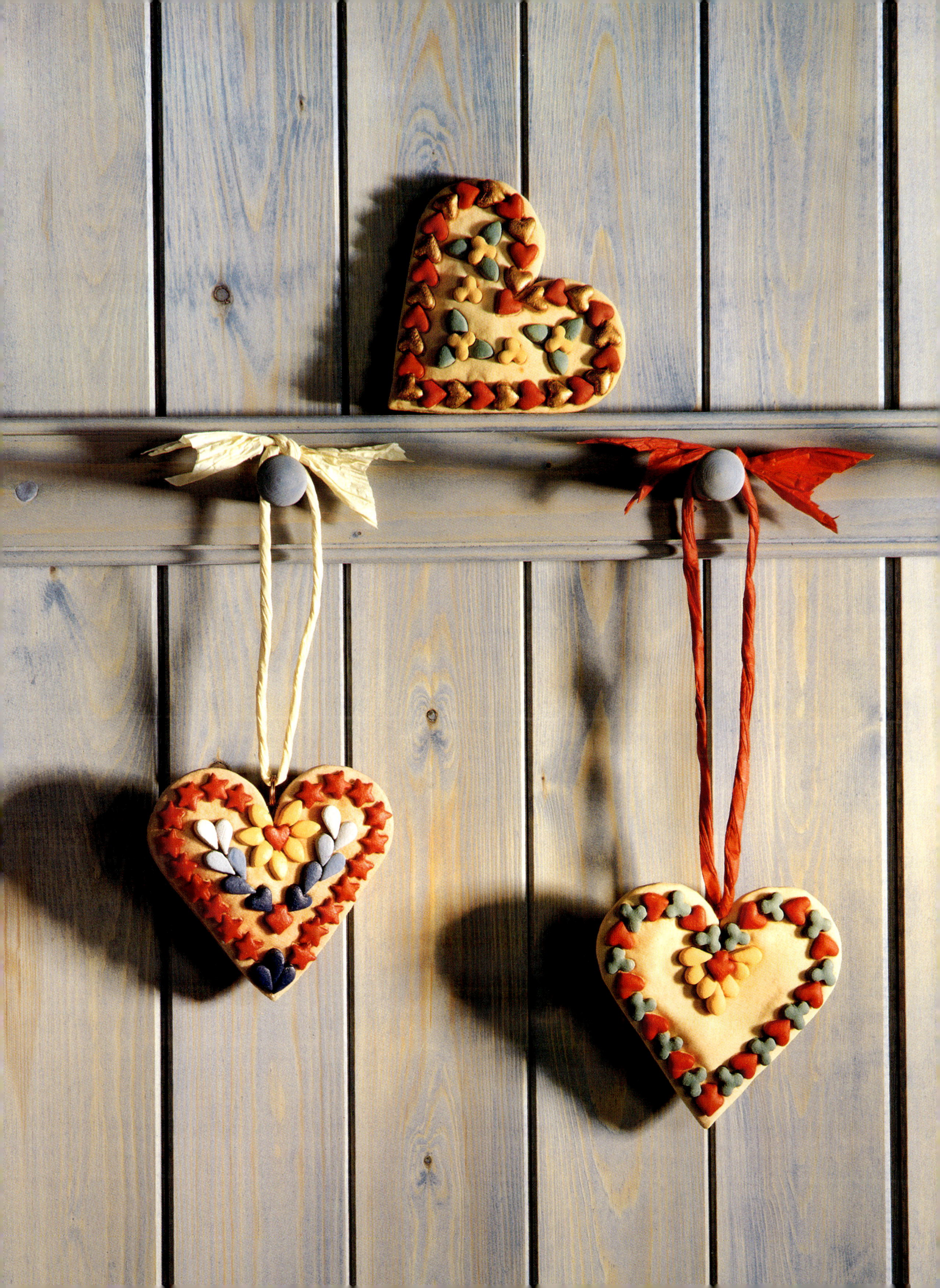

Checkered Heart

This eye-catching heart is simple to make, and looks very effective hung with several others in a group on a wall or in a window area, where they will sway gently in the breeze. They also make delightful gifts, especially for Valentine's Day or a birthday.

YOU WILL NEED
(to make 3 hearts)

~

pencil and tracing paper

scissors

1 quantity salt dough (see page 16)

rolling pin

baking parchment (parchment paper)

small, sharp knife

modelling tool (optional)

dressmaking pin or thin skewer

3 gold paperclips

wire-cutters

baking tray

acrylic gesso or matt emulsion (flat latex) paint

paintbrushes

acrylic or craft paint

polyurethane matt varnish

coloured raffia

1. Size the smaller template on page 154, transfer to tracing paper and cut out. Roll the dough out flat on baking parchment (parchment paper) to a thickness of approximately 3/8 in (1 cm), place the template on the dough and carefully cut around it with a sharp knife. Mark the squares on the dough with a dressmaking pin or thin skewer.

2. Neaten the cut edge of the heart by patting with a moistened finger to round and smooth it. Using a knife or modelling tool, indent lines on the heart, following the pricked marks, leaning the knife or tool first towards you and then away from you to create rounded edges on either side of the lines. This creates a cushioned look.

~ *Checkered Heart* ~

This heart takes its inspiration from traditional Scandinavian folk art. The dough squares are formed by deep indentations, although they give the impression of being separate pieces (far right).

~ *Wall Ornaments* ~

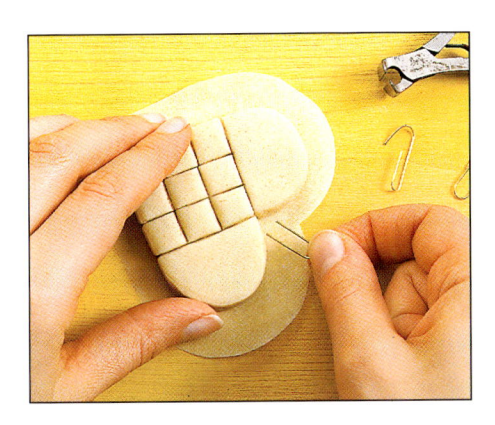

3. Snip a gold paperclip in half with wire-cutters and insert it into the top of the heart to form a hanging loop. Re-roll the remaining dough and repeat Steps 1–3 to make 2 or more hearts. Transfer the hearts, on the parchment, to a baking tray, and bake in the oven at 250°F/ 120°C/Gas ½ for 9 hours until hard. Allow to cool.

4. Paint on an undercoat of acrylic gesso or matt emulsion (flat latex) paint, and leave to dry. Paint the hearts with cherry red acrylic or craft paint, leaving alternate squares plain. When dry, apply 5 coats of matt varnish, allowing the varnish to dry between each coat. Thread a 16 in (40 cm) length of raffia through each loop, make a knot, and tie the ends into a decorative bow. ▸

~ *Wall Ornaments* ~

~ *Heart Labels* ~

In addition to the textured Scandinavian-style chequered hearts (left and right), salt dough is excellent for making flat plaques which can be decorated on one side and painted plain white on the reverse. If left unvarnished, a message can be written on the plain side, and the heart can be used as a pretty gift tag (below).

~ Wall Ornaments ~

112

Flying Angel

This charming angel would look pretty on any wall, and can be painted in the colours of your choice to match its surroundings. The basic angel shape can be varied in endless ways to create different models.

YOU WILL NEED

~

tracing paper and pencil
baking parchment (parchment paper)
1 quantity salt dough (see page 16)
modelling tool
dressmaking pin
small heart-shaped cutter
paperclip
wire-cutters
baking tray
acrylic gesso or matt emulsion (flat latex) paint
paintbrushes
acrylic or craft paints
polyurethane matt varnish

1. Size the template on page 154 and transfer to an 8 in (20 cm) square of baking parchment (parchment paper). This will be the guide for assembling the various parts of the angel. First make the wings. Roll a sausage of dough and curl the end. Lay it on to the traced outline at the top of the left wing. Make 3 similar sausages, each getting progressively smaller. Gently press the sausages into place.

Repeat the process to make the second wing. Roll a 1¼ in (3 cm) ball of dough to form the head, and flatten it slightly. Moisten the inner edge of the right wing and place the head in position.

2. Mould a body shape, following the outline on the template. Moisten the top edges of the shape with a little water, and join to the head and wings. Smooth the edges with a modelling tool. The angel's hair is formed from small coils of dough arranged round the head. Make as many of these as you need, varying the sizes slightly, then moisten the head and press the coils gently into place. Mark the eyes and mouth with a dressmaking pin. ▶

~ Wall Ornaments ~

~ *Flower Angel* ~

Experiment by using just the head and wings, made in the same way as the larger angels, to produce small angelic busts (above).

~ *Celebration Angel* ~

Make this gently swathed angel for a special occasion, a wedding or Christening memento, perhaps (below).

3. Use the small cutter to cut out a heart from the remaining dough to decorate the dress. Moisten the underside of the heart and press it into place. Make the feet from pea-sized balls of dough. Flatten the balls and press them into triangles, then join to the body. Snip the paperclip in half with wire-cutters and press it into the top of the angel's head.

Transfer the angel, on the baking parchment (parchment paper) to a baking tray, and bake in the oven at 250°F/120°C/Gas ½ for 10 hours. Allow to cool. Paint on an undercoat of acrylic gesso or matt emulsion (flat latex) paint and leave to dry. Paint the model with acrylic or craft paints, leave to dry, then apply 5 coats of matt varnish, allowing the varnish to dry between each coat.

~ *Flying Angel* ~

This angel has charming curly hair, a cheeky smile and a heart emblazoned on his chest (right). Once you have mastered the basic template you can create all sorts of delightful cherub variations.

~ Wall Ornaments ~

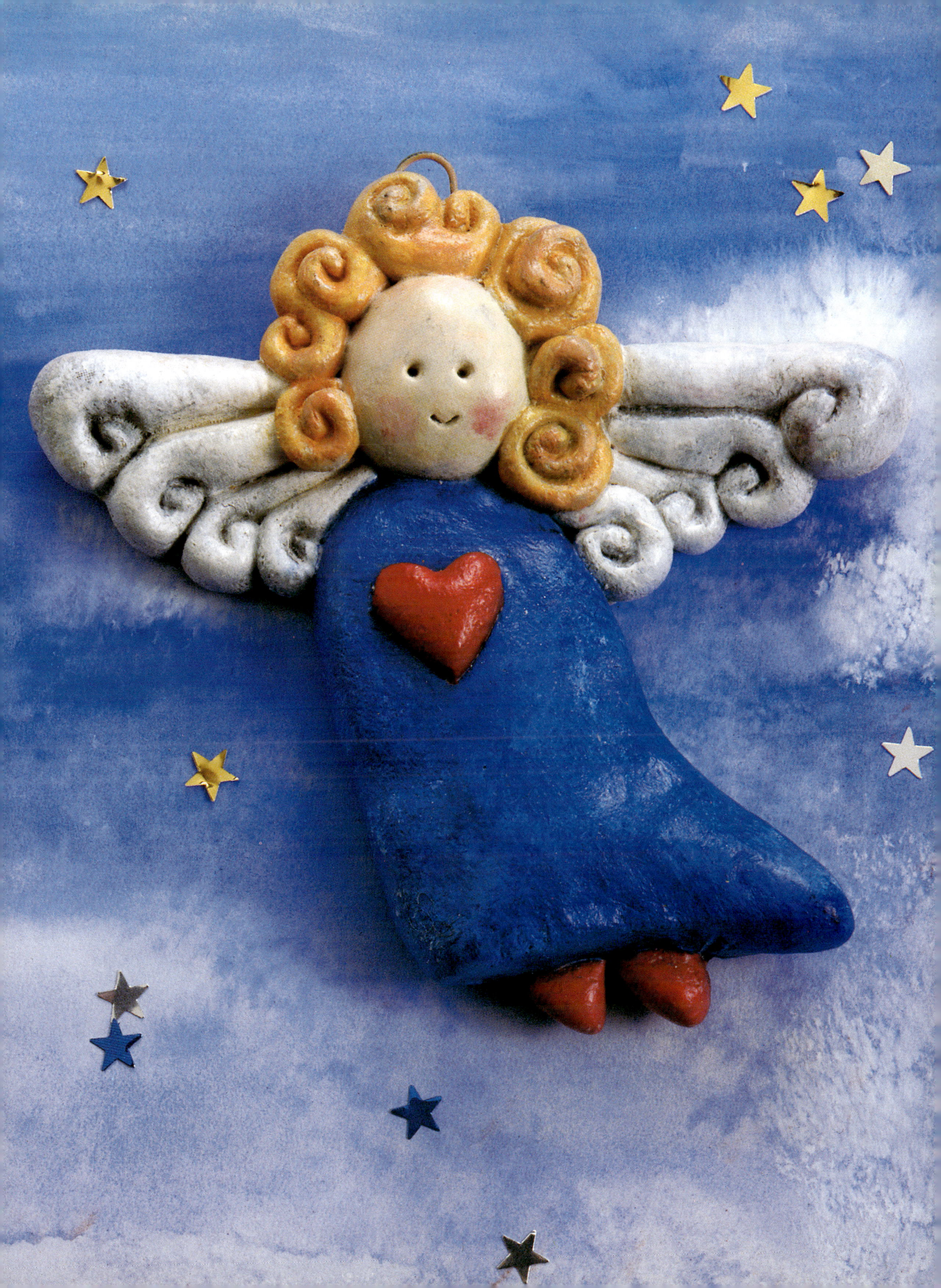

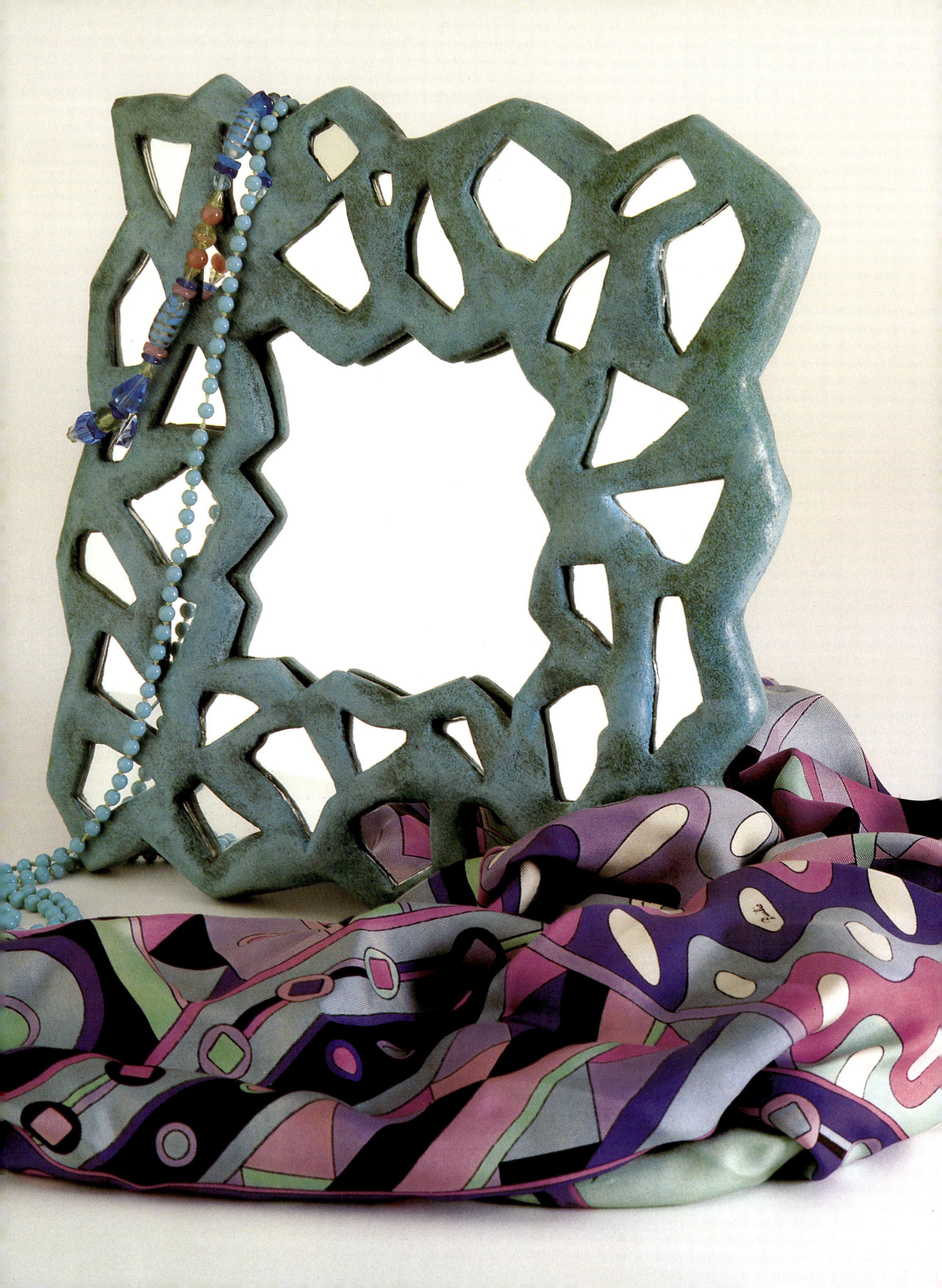

Mosaic Mirror

The cool blue of this mosaic mirror is obtained from food colouring and evokes a relaxed and tranquil mood. The decorative technique used here involves the smashing of mirror tiles into fragments and then embedding them in the dough. You can either hang the mirror on the wall by inserting wire hooks on the back, or make a stand as described.

YOU WILL NEED

~

tracing paper and pencil

scissors

4 x quantity salt dough (see page 16) – you will find this easier to make in batches

blue food colouring

rolling pin

baking parchment (parchment paper)

three 6 in (15 cm) mirror tiles

small, sharp knife

old towel

hammer

baking tray

baking foil

masking tape

fine-grade sandpaper

polyurethane satin varnish

paintbrush

~ *Mosaic Mirror* ~

This exciting mirror design (left) allows multiple views of your reflection, with the blue-coloured dough setting off each embedded shard of glass. The original brightness of the blue colouring will fade over time.

1. Size the stand and mirror-frame templates on page 155 and transfer to tracing paper. Cut out the templates, including the centre of the frame. Mix the food colouring into the dough, following Step 1 on page 17. Divide the dough in half and roll each half out flat on a piece of baking parchment (parchment paper) to an approximate thickness of 3/8 in (1 cm). Press a mirror tile centrally on to one piece of the rolled dough.

2. Use the template to cut out the mirror frame, including the centre, on the second piece of rolled dough. Carefully lift the frame, on the parchment, and place it face-down on the first piece, positioning the cut-out centre over the mirror tile. Peel off the parchment. Cut away the upper section of dough around the outer edges of the frame. Pat the edges with a knife to neaten. Smooth the dough with a moistened finger to even out the surface. ▶

~ *Wall Ornaments* ~

~ *Mirror of the Heart* ~

Here a natural dough base in the shape of a pierced heart holds within it a mosaic design of mirrors and old china. The blue cabochon in the centre picks up the blue in the pieces of china, while the whiteness of the dough emphasizes the reflection of light in the mirror. To create this pattern, choose long, thin shards of broken mirror and embed them in the dough so that they radiate out from the central "jewel". Fill in the remaining areas with pieces of co-ordinating china, adding smaller bits in the outer areas that remain empty. Smooth down the dough around the pieces with a moistened finger and bake on a baking tray until hard. The mirror and china pieces will withstand the heat well.

3. Wrap the remaining mirror tiles in an old towel and smash with a hammer (throw the towel away after). With care, arrange the fragments on the frame, then press into the dough. Smooth the dough over the mirror edges with a moistened finger. Roll the remaining dough out flat on baking parchment (parchment paper) to a thickness of ⅝ in (1.5 cm), and cut out the stand, using the template. Bake the frame in the oven at 250°F/120°C/Gas ½ for 24 hours and the stand for 12 hours. Allow to cool.

4. To make the stand, moisten the shorter of the long stand edges, and smear with dough. With the mirror face-down, dampen the back along the centre and press the stand on top. Spread more dough along the join. Support with scrunched baking foil held in place with masking tape, and return to the oven for 3 hours. Allow to cool, remove the foil and tape, then sand carefully along the join. Finally, apply 5 coats of satin varnish to the mirror, using a fine brush to extend the varnish around the edges of the mirror fragments.

~ *Wall Ornaments* ~

Framed Fish

The bright colours of this fine fish lend a contemporary air and a touch of humour to the tradition of displaying prized fish catches in glass-fronted boxes. The blue-green background, some sprinkled sand and a few scattered sea shells and starfish complete the marine theme.

YOU WILL NEED

~

1 quantity salt dough (see page 16)
rolling pin
baking parchment (parchment paper)
tracing paper and pencil
scissors
small, sharp knife
dressmaking pin
teaspoon
baking tray
watercolour paints
paintbrushes
ceramic tile or old plate
polyurethane satin varnish
watercolour paper
box frame measuring approximately 8 x 12 in (20 x 30 cm)
masking tape
thick card (cardboard) or wood
wood glue
wood block, 2 x 3 x 3/4 in (5 x 7.5 x 2 cm)
sand
shells and starfish

1. Roll the dough out flat on baking parchment (parchment paper) to a thickness of 3/8 in (1 cm). Size the fish template on page 156, transfer to tracing paper and cut out. Place the template on the dough and cut around the outer edges with a knife. Remove the template, then pat the edges of the fish to round and smooth them.

2. Replace the template and prick along the lines through the paper on to the dough with a pin to transfer the design. Lightly moisten the fish shape all over and indent the lines with the knife tip. Leaning the blade towards you, work along the line again, then lean the knife away from you to make an inverted division around the head. ▶

~ Wall Ornaments ~

119

3. Press a teaspoon on to the dough to mark the scales, spacing them evenly over the fish's body. Roll a small piece of dough out flat to a thickness of ¼ in (5 mm). Cut out a fin shape, and pat the cut edges to round them.

~ Framed Fish ~

This realistic-looking trophy is of course a trompe'l'œil *masterpiece in salt dough (above). Boxes of this sort can be found quite easily in craft shops, and decorated to fit the subject.*

~ Wall Ornaments ~

~ *Family of Seahorses* ~

These are an excellent subject for marine models: several coats of gloss varnish give the creatures the appearance of being wet, while a slightly tinted varnish can add extra definition.

4. Moisten the underside of the fin and place it on the fish. Indent the markings on the fin with the knife tip. Cut a fringe around the outer lines of the fish, and cut the fringe ends at an angle. Mould a ³⁄₈ in (1 cm) diameter ball for the eye, and form it into an egg shape. Flatten and press to the head, then flatten a smaller ball and press on top. Transfer the fish, on the parchment, to a baking tray, and bake in the oven at 250°F/120°C/Gas ½ for 9 hours. Allow to cool.

5. Paint the fish with watercolour paints, mixing the colours on a ceramic tile or old plate. Indian yellow, cadmium orange, permanent rose and permanent magenta were used for the fish shown here; Chinese white and ivory black were used for the eye. Leave to dry, then apply 5 coats of satin varnish. To line the box, cut pieces of watercolour paper slightly larger than the sides, base, top and back of the box frame. Tape the paper to thick card (cardboard) or wood.

6. Moisten the paper with a large paintbrush, then paint with watercolour paints, blending the colours together while the paint is still wet. Leave to dry, then peel off the tape and cut the paper to fit the sides, base, top and back of the box frame. Glue the paper inside the frame and smooth down.

7. Glue the wood block centrally to the back of the fish, and then centrally to the back of the box frame. Spread a thin film of glue randomly on the base of the frame, sprinkle on some sand and leave to dry. Shake off the excess sand and glue a few shells and starfish inside. Assemble the frame and hang up.

~ *Wall Ornaments* ~

Wall Clock

Paint the clock in colours to co-ordinate with the décor of your room. The clock fittings can be bought from most craft and specialist clock shops. Remember that salt dough is vulnerable in a damp atmosphere, so, if you hang the clock in the kitchen, make sure that it is away from the stove and not hanging above the sink.

1. Roll the dough out flat on a lightly floured chopping board or baking parchment (parchment paper) to a thickness of ⅝ in (1.5 cm). Place a plate on the salt dough and cut around it with a sharp knife. Remove the excess dough. Find the centre of the circle and pierce a hole with a skewer, large enough to fit the clock mechanism.

YOU WILL NEED
~

2 x quantity salt dough (see page 16)

rolling pin

chopping board and flour for dusting

baking parchment (parchment paper)

plate

small, sharp knife

skewer

baking tray

acrylic gesso or matt emulsion (flat latex) paint

paintbrushes

acrylic or craft paints

polyurethane matt varnish

clock mechanism and hands

~ **Wall Clock** ~

This dotty dough clock is simple to make, using an ordinary plate as the template. Round, flat models such as this are easy to make as they bake evenly - remember not to make them larger in circumference than the oven shelf!

2. Roll 4 pieces of dough, each with a ⅝ in (1.5 cm) diameter, into balls. Flatten the balls, moisten them and stick on the clock at the 4 quarterly points. Decorate the outer rim of the clock with squares of salt dough, sticking them on with a dab of water and smoothing the joins with a moistened finger. Roll more small balls of dough, flatten them and stick at random over the clock face and rim with a little water.

~ Wall Ornaments ~

3. Transfer the clock, on parchment, to a baking tray, and bake in the oven at 250°F/120°C/Gas ½ for 1½ hours. Paint on an undercoat of acrylic gesso or matt emulsion (flat latex) paint. Leave to dry.

4. Paint the clock with an assortment of colours, adding details with a fine paintbrush, and leave it to dry. Apply 5 coats of matt varnish, allowing the varnish to dry between each coat.

5. Attach the mechanism and hands following the manufacturer's instructions, and hang up the clock.

~ *Wall Ornaments* ~

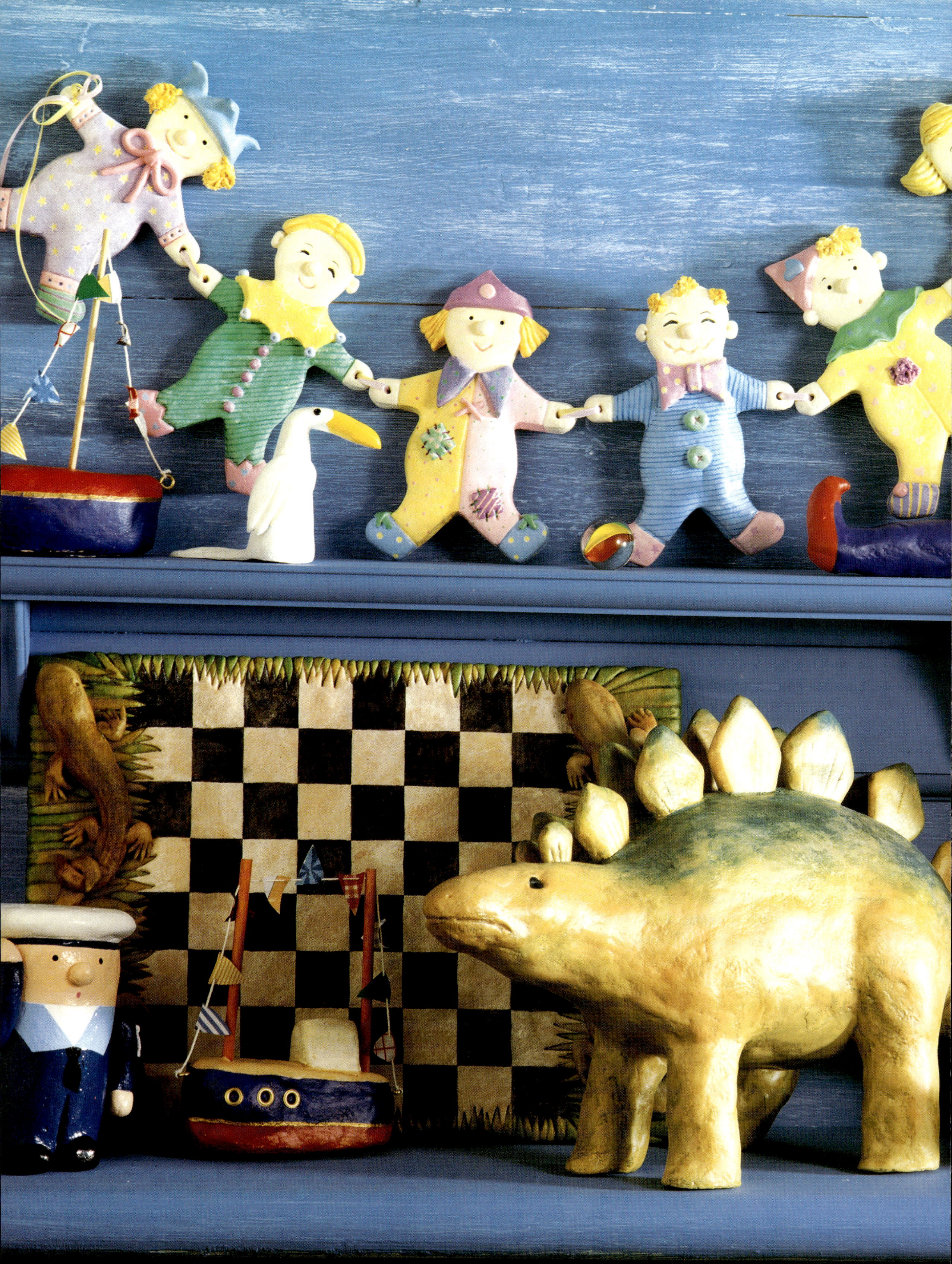

Toys, Games & Animals

Not only is salt dough an ideal play substance for young children when unbaked, but it is also well suited to the production of toys and games when fired. It is a fairly hardy substance if moulded thickly enough and it can be painted in attractive colours, perfect for toys or nursery ornaments. Fabric decorations can be added to create sails on boats, or doll's clothes, for example. The dough's versatility means that both modern and traditional designs can be adapted for modelling, and toys are the perfect items for experimentation as the results are always sure to please; any anomalies become part of the design.

~ A Nursery Shelf ~

This collection of brightly decorated salt dough toys brings together ideal distractions for a child: puppets, dinosaurs, games, dolls and boats.

Flotilla of Boats

Set sail with a colourful group of weather-beaten boats reminiscent of traditional nautical models. As the boats are three-dimensional, they are modelled first from foil which is then covered with a layer of salt dough. Metal studs or brass eyelets for portholes add a finishing touch.

YOU WILL NEED

~

baking foil

masking tape

baking parchment
(parchment paper)

1 quantity salt dough (see page 16)

small, sharp knife

metal studs or eyelets (optional)

screw eyes (optional)

skewer

fine wood dowelling

baking tray

acrylic gesso or matt emulsion
(flat latex) paint

paintbrushes

acrylic or craft paints

burnt sienna Indian ink (optional)

fine-grade sandpaper

polyurethane matt varnish

PVA medium

fabric scraps

scissors

craft knife

thick thread

large-eyed sewing needle

1. Begin by scrunching a piece of baking foil loosely into a ball. Mould it into the boat shape by pressing the foil against a hard surface. Mould a smaller piece of foil into a cube to represent a cabin, and stick it to the boat with masking tape. Working on a sheet of baking parchment (parchment paper), take a piece of the dough and press it around the foil to a thickness of approximately ¼ in (5 mm).

2. It is not necessary to cover the underside of the boat with dough at this stage. Smooth the surface of the dough with a moistened finger and cut away any excess dough with a sharp knife.

If the boat you are designing has a cabin, gently press metal studs or eyelets into each side of the boat. Insert screw eyes into the ends of the boat if you wish to hoist some pennants.

~ Toys, Games & Animals ~

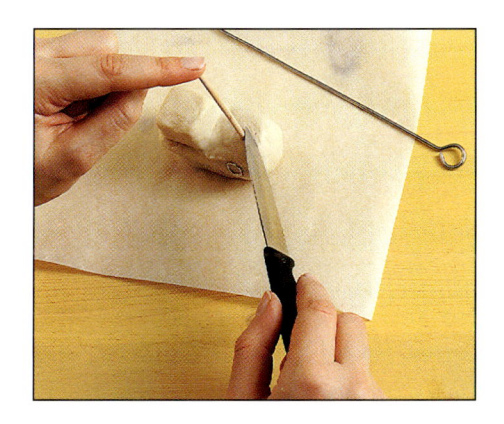

~ Flotilla of Boats ~

This convoy of brightly painted boats is perfect for a child to make – the technique is simple and the decorating great fun, especially the choosing of the fabric for the flags and pennants. The boats make an excellent wintertime distraction when it may be too cold to venture out to play. Cars could be made using the same foil support, with flattened dough balls stuck along the sides to form wheels. As with the boats, a whole collection could be made, and in no time at all the house will be full of salt dough vehicles in convoys and traffic jams.

3. To add a mast, pierce a hole in the top of the boat with a skewer, then push a length of dowelling into the hole. Gently press the dough around the dowelling to hold it steady. Repeat the whole process to make as many boats as you wish. Transfer the boats, on the parchment, to a baking tray, and bake in the oven at 250°F/120°C/Gas ½ for 4½ hours. Upturn the boats and press a layer of dough to the undersides, then return to the oven for a further 4½ hours. Allow to cool.

4. Paint the boats with an undercoat of acrylic gesso or matt emulsion (flat latex) paint, and leave to dry. Paint on acrylic or craft paints in bright colours, and paint the masts with burnt sienna Indian ink or leave plain. Gently sand the boats to add a realistic touch of wear and tear. Apply 5 coats of matt varnish, allowing the varnish to dry between each coat. Paint a layer of PVA medium on to scraps of fabric to make pennants – the medium will stiffen the fabric and prevent fraying.

~ Toys, Games & Animals ~

5. Cut out small rectangles for flags and triangles for pennants. Glue a flag around the top of each mast using PVA medium. Use a craft knife to cut a slit across the top of the masts of boats that will have a string of pennants.

6. Tie a length of thick thread to one screw eye, thread it on to a large-eyed needle and insert through the pennants. Slot the thread into the slit in the mast and tie on to the other screw eye.

~ Flag-Flying Tug ~

Decorate the boats so that each is an individual member of the fleet. Here a metal star-shaped stud is a striking and official-looking emblem with a flag to match.

~ Toys, Games & Animals ~

128

Garland of Clowns

This amusing row of clowns is easy enough for children to make. The clown shapes are cut out using a pastry cutter, and can be decorated as simply or as lavishly as you wish. The clowns are all threaded together on fine ribbons, and make a fun and colourful toy.

YOU WILL NEED
~
1 quantity salt dough (see page 16)
rolling pin
baking parchment
(parchment paper)
gingerbread-man pastry cutter
thick needle
dressmaking pin (optional)
sieve (sifter)
small, sharp knife
baking tray
acrylic gesso or matt emulsion
(flat latex) paint
paintbrushes
Indian inks
ceramic tile or old plate
polyurethane matt varnish
fine ribbons

1. Roll the dough out flat on baking parchment (parchment paper) to a thickness of 3/8 in (1 cm), then press the pastry cutter into the dough to cut six characters. Roll balls of dough for the clowns' noses, each 5/16 in (8 mm) in diameter. Moisten the faces and press the noses in place. Draw eyes and mouths with a thick needle or indent them with the head of a pin.

2. Use the needle to pierce a hole through the "hands" large enough to thread through ribbons. Press the needle across the "wrists", then use its point to draw details such as seams and trouser bottoms. Smooth any rough or bumpy areas with a moistened finger. ▶

~ Toys, Games & Animals ~

129

3. Re-roll the remaining dough out flat to a thickness of 1/8 in (3 mm) and cut out hats, collars, bow-ties, braces and patches. A frilled edge can be given to a collar by squeezing the lower edge of the dough shape and gently stretching it. Moisten the components and press in place.

~ Garland of Clowns ~

Each clown has a differently painted outfit within a certain range of colours. This produces a pleasing combination of co-ordinating colourways. Add more clowns to the garland to decorate a wall or doorframe.

~ Toys, Games & Animals ~

130

4. Moisten small balls of dough and press to the models as buttons and ears. Indent buttons and ears with a pin head or the thick needle. To make frizzy hair and pompons, press small pieces of dough through a sieve (sifter). Cut off the resulting shreds and gently press in place. ▶

~ *Toys, Games & Animals* ~

~ Happy Trio ~

The clowns are equally effective when left unpainted. Bake as usual and then coat with a matt varnish. The natural dough emphasizes the indentations of the design without the need for any added colour.

5. To make straight hair, mould dough into suitable shapes, moisten the head and press the hair in position. Indent the hair with the tip of a knife. Roll thin sausages of dough as shoelaces. Moisten the clowns and carefully arrange the laces in place. Indent "stitches" on the patches with the knife tip.

Transfer the clowns, on the parchment, to a baking tray, and bake in the oven at 250°F/120°C/Gas ½ for 12 hours.

6. Allow to cool, then undercoat the models with acrylic gesso or matt emulsion (flat latex) paint. Paint the clowns with Indian inks mixed with the gesso on a ceramic tile or old plate to lighten the colours. Add details with a fine paintbrush. Apply 5 coats of matt varnish, allowing the varnish to dry between each coat. When dry, thread the clowns on to two lengths of fine ribbon. Tie the ribbons together in a bow to secure.

~ Toys, Games & Animals ~

Checker Board

Realistic lizards scamper around the edges of this unusual checker board. It is simple to make, *and, when displayed on a table, will provide a talking point even when it is not in use!*

YOU WILL NEED

~

2 x quantity salt dough (see page 16)
rolling pin
baking parchment (parchment paper)
small, sharp knife
ruler
pencil and paper
scissors
dressmaking pins
baking tray
shells
watercolour paints
paintbrushes
ceramic tile or old plate
polyurethane satin varnish

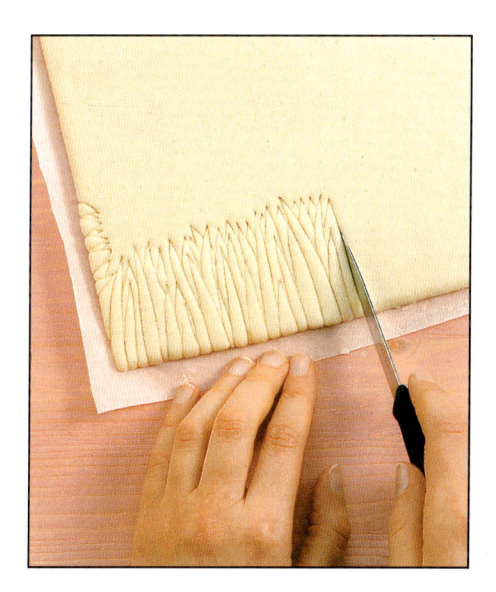

1. Roll the dough out flat on baking parchment (parchment paper) to a thickness of 3/8 in (1 cm). Using a knife and ruler, cut a rectangle measuring 12¼ x 8½ in (31 x 22 cm) for the board. Pat the cut edges with a moistened finger to round them. Cut a square of paper measuring 8 x 8 in (20 x 20 cm). Place the square centrally on the dough, and mark the corners and centre of each side with dressmaking pins. Remove the paper.

2. Moisten the edges of the rectangle and draw grasses on the dough with the tip of a knife, allowing the grass tips to overlap the area of the square. Remove the pins as you work. Roll 2 sausages of dough for the lizards, each 3¼ in (8 cm) long and ¾ in (2 cm) thick. Roll one end of each sausage to narrow it for a tail. ▶

~ Toys, Games & Animals ~

3. Draw a rectangle measuring 8½ x 2¼ in (22 x 5.5 cm) on baking parchment (parchment paper). Arrange the lizards within the parchment rectangle, linking the tails together. Squeeze the tail tips to point them. Squeeze the wide end of the lizards to point the heads slightly, and press each side of the lizards to narrow them below the heads.

4. Roll four ½ in (1.25 cm) diameter balls of dough for legs for each lizard. Roll into sausages and bend in half. Moisten one end and press against the lizard, smoothing over the join with a moistened finger. Flatten the extending ends and cut into 4 toes. Indent the eyes with a pin head. Repeat the process to make 2 more lizards.

5. Bake the dough rectangle and the lizards at 250°F/120°C/Gas ½ for 1 hour. Allow to cool, then smear the undersides of the lizards with dough. Press on the rectangle, then continue baking for a further 9 hours. Meanwhile, roll twenty-four ½ in (1.25 cm) diameter balls of dough for counters. Flatten the balls and emboss with shells. Bake for 4 hours.

6. Paint the lizards, grass and counters with watercolour paints, mixing the colours on a ceramic tile or an old plate. Paint the centre of the board white. Divide this area into 8 rows of 8 squares, each 1 x 1 in (2.5 x 2.5 cm), allowing the outer squares to extend into the foliage. Paint alternate squares black. Apply 5 coats of satin varnish.

~ *Checker Board* ~

These beautiful, realistic-looking lizards lie along the board's edge, their tails gently entwined (above). Salt dough produces durable playing counters; the texture on their tops is produced with shells pressed into the dough.

~ Toys, Games & Animals ~

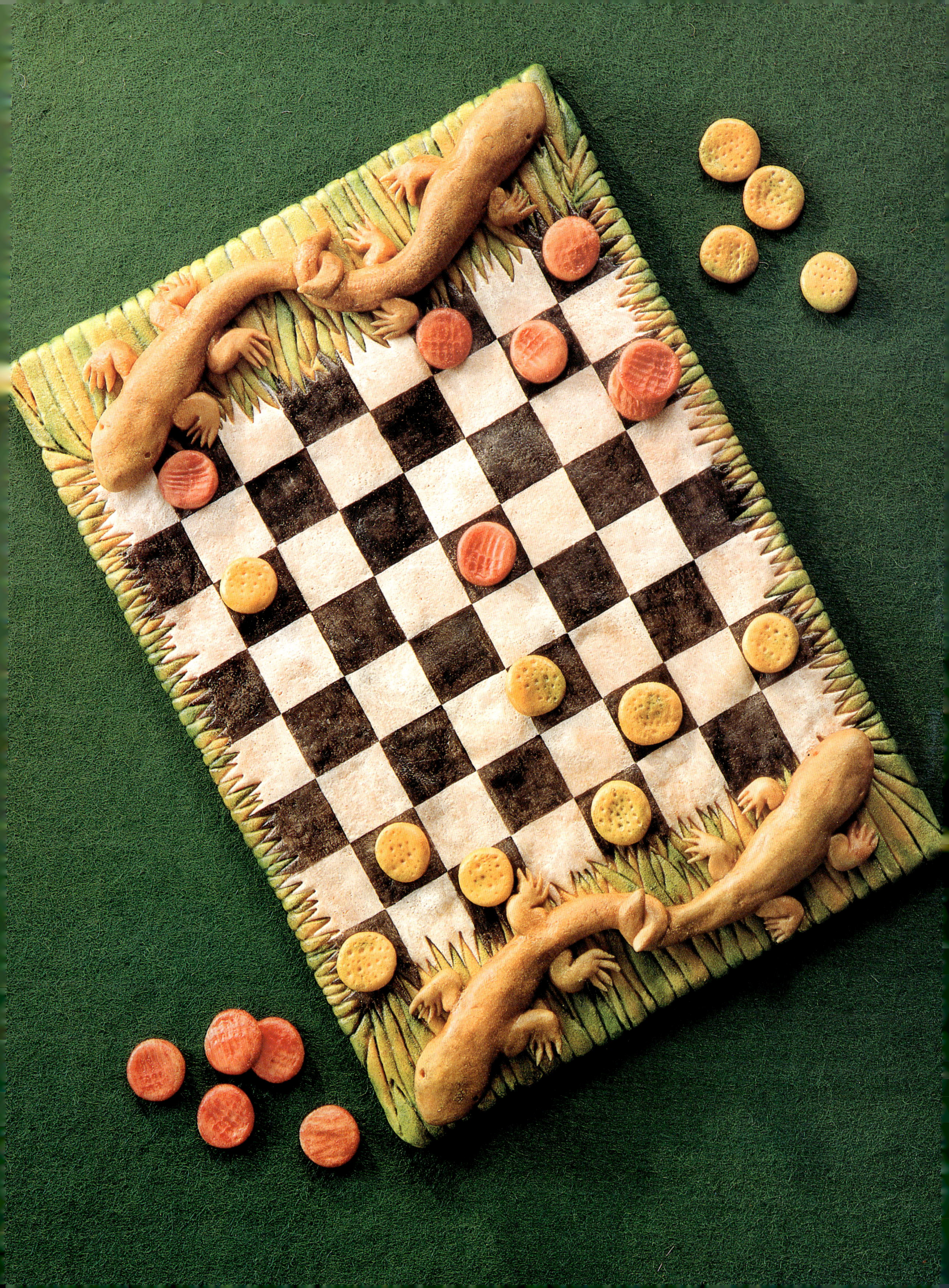

Dinosaur

Dinosaurs are fascinating for children and adults alike – this magnificent model is a stegosaurus. The simple method used to make the dinosaur, of modelling on a structure of chicken wire, can easily be adapted to make a variety of unusual creatures.

YOU WILL NEED

~

wire-cutters
small-gauge chicken wire
pliers
tracing paper and pencil
scissors
2 x quantity salt dough (see page 16)
rolling pin
baking parchment (parchment paper)
small, sharp knife
baking tray
baking foil
masking tape
2 glass beads for eyes
watercolour paints
paintbrushes
ceramic tile or old plate
polyurethane matt varnish

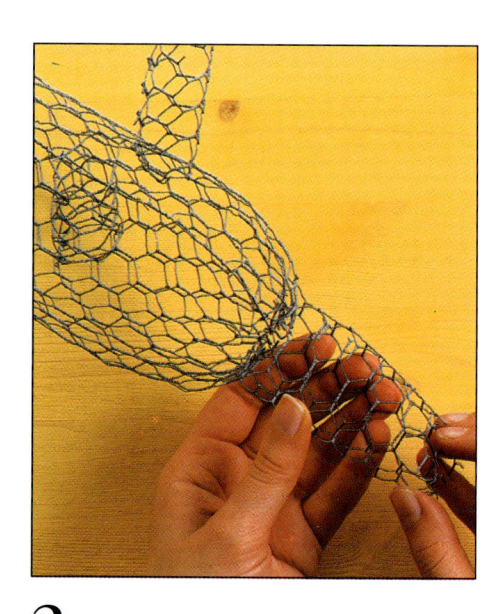

1. Use wire-cutters to cut a 11½ x 9½ in (29 x 24 cm) rectangle from chicken wire for the body. Bend the wire into a tube, with the short ends meeting. Hook the meeting edges together with pliers to hold the shape. Squeeze the ends of the wire to form the body into an oval. Use wire-cutters to cut a 10 x 5½ in (25 x 14 cm) rectangle for the tail and a 5½ x 4 in (14 x 10 cm) rectangle for the head from chicken wire. Bend the tail into a tube with the short ends meeting. Hook the meeting edges together with pliers.

2. Use wire-cutters to cut 4 rectangles of chicken wire for the legs, each measuring 3¼ x 2¾ in (8.5 x 7 cm). Bend the rectangles into tubes with the short ends meeting. Hook the meeting edges together with pliers. Position the legs under the body and hook the cut ends into the body. Bend the tail around the side of the body, squeezing the open end to taper it. Squeeze the open end of the head to narrow it. Check that the model will fit in the oven, bearing in mind that it will have plates and spines on top.

~ *Toys, Games & Animals* ~

3. Size the templates of the plates on page 156, transfer to tracing paper and cut out the shapes. Roll the dough out flat on baking parchment (parchment paper) to a thickness of ¼ in (5 mm). Cut out 2 size A plates, 8 size B plates and 4 each of sizes C, D and E plates. Pat the cut edges to round them and indent veins with the tip of a knife. ▶

~ Dinosaur ~

The ponderous character of this stegosaurus comes over clearly. When baked, the salt dough forms a surface that closely resembles that of the skin of a dinosaur as we suppose it to have been. This is the perfect model for children to make, and perhaps alter the design to form a whole collection.

~ Toys, Games & Animals ~

4. Roll 4 sausages of dough, each 1¾ in (4.5 cm) long, for spines. Squeeze one end of each sausage to narrow it, then bend into a curve. Transfer the plates and spines, on the parchment, to a baking tray, and bake in the oven at 250°F/120°C/Gas ½ for 3 hours. Meanwhile, tear strips of baking foil and bind them around the armature, squeezing the foil to fit around the wire. Stick the foil in place with masking tape. Start to spread dough along the top of the dinosaur, building it up on the model's back.

5. Insert the plates into the dough in pairs and facing outwards. Start with the largest in the centre then work outwards to the smallest, taping the pairs together with masking tape to hold them upright. Insert the spines in the same way on the tail. Bake for 2 hours, then add more dough to the model.

~ *Warthog* ~

Another example of a smooth-skinned creature built over wire for strength and support.

6. Embed beads for eyes in the dough, and mark the mouth and nostrils with a knife. Return the model to the oven and bake for a further 2 hours. Continue smoothing on more dough and baking until the dinosaur is covered with dough and thoroughly hardened.

Allow to cool completely, then paint the model with watercolour paints, mixing the colours on a ceramic tile or old plate. Finally, apply 5 coats of matt varnish, allowing the varnish to dry thoroughly between each coat.

~ *Toys, Games & Animals* ~

Animal Finger Puppets

Guaranteed to entertain and easy to make, these colourful and amusing finger puppets are constructed over cardboard cones. Once you have mastered the technique, you could make a whole range of comical and exotic characters, and perhaps even a simple theatre.

YOU WILL NEED

~

tracing paper and pencil
thin card (cardboard)
scissors
masking tape
1 quantity salt dough (see page 16)
small, sharp knife
pastry wheel
2 wooden cocktail sticks (toothpicks)
rolling pin
6 small and 4 slightly larger glass beads for eyes
toy-making whiskers (available from craft shops)
baking parchment (parchment paper)
baking tray
acrylic gesso or matt emulsion (flat latex) paint
paintbrushes
acrylic or craft paints
small natural sponge
polyurethane satin varnish
stranded cotton embroidery thread
scrap of brown long-haired fur fabric
all-purpose household glue

1. To make a seagull, dragon, fox, crocodile and giraffe, first trace the finger puppet templates on page 156 to the size required. Place the tracings face-down on to thin card (cardboard) and re-draw to transfer the outlines. You will need 5 basic puppet shapes (the giraffe is the only one without the main tail shape), 1 separate fox and dragon tail, 2 dragon's wings and 2 bird's wings. Cut out the pieces. Bend the puppets into cone shapes and stick the overlapped edges together with masking tape. Then, bend over each point at the fold line to form the head.

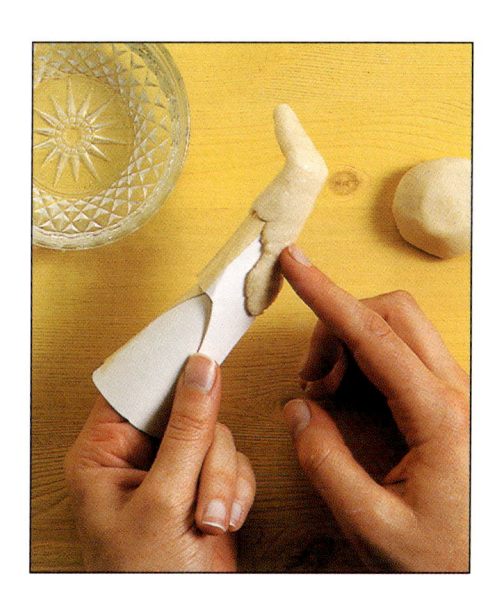

2. To support the puppets, cut a quarter-circle of card (cardboard) with a radius of 2½ in (6cm). Bend it into a cone and stick the overlapped edges together with masking tape. Support the puppets on the cones, and smear on the dough, blending it evenly with a moistened finger. ▶

~ Toys, Games & Animals ~

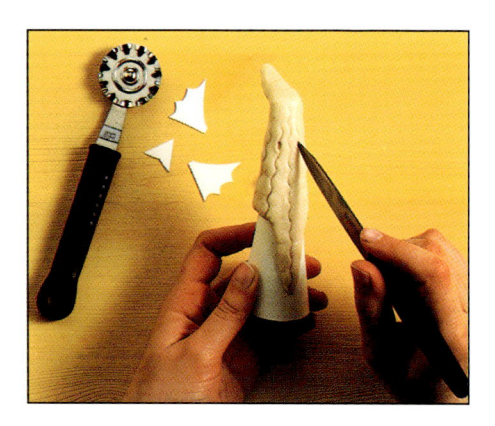

3. To decorate the dragon, make a wiggly pattern with a knife or pastry wheel, and then cut two slits on its back for inserting the wings. For the giraffe, cut two 3/8 in (1cm) lengths from a cocktail stick (toothpick), and insert into the top of its head. Pierce a hole in the base for inserting the tail. Press on ears, beads for eyes, and a mouth.

4. To make the fox, first cut 2in (5cm) lengths of toy-making whiskers, moisten the fox's snout and carefully place the whiskers on top. Roll a small ball of dough for a nose and press to the top of the snout, sandwiching the whiskers. Cut out and press on ears, and 2 small beads for eyes. For the seagull, use the templates to mould 2 wing shapes and secure on to the sides of the model with moistened dough. Press on 2 small beads for eyes.

~ *Toys, Games & Animals* ~

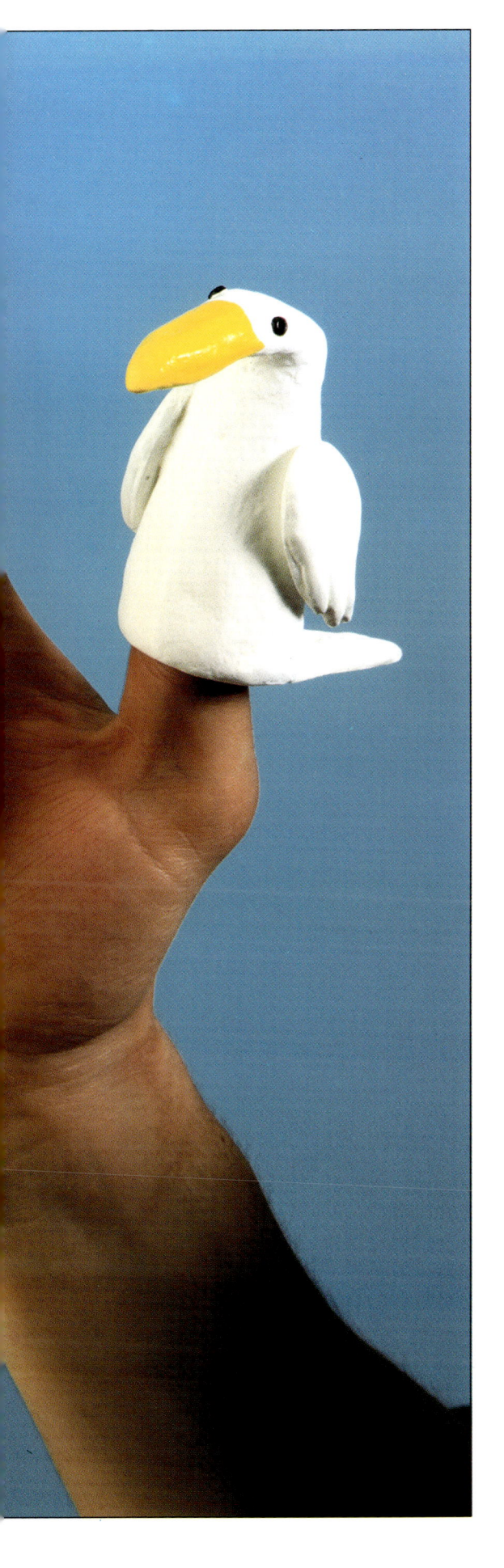

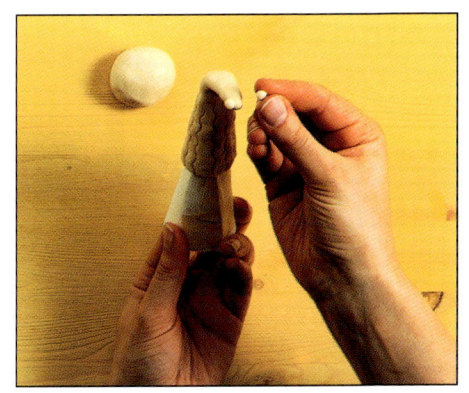

5. To finish the dragon, roll 2 small balls as nostrils and press in place, indenting with a cocktail stick (toothpick). Roll two 3/8 in (1cm) balls of dough, press in 2 larger beads, and press on to the dragon's head as eyes. Indent a mouthline. Roll out dough thinly and cut out 2 wings and a tail; these will be added after the first baking. To make the crocodile, create nostrils, eyes and mouth in exactly the same way as for the dragon. Stand all the pieces on baking parchment (parchment paper) on a baking tray and bake in the oven at 250°F/120°C/Gas ½ for 3 hours. Gently fold the dragon's wings along the "veins", moisten the ends and the corresponding slits on the body, and press into place. Moisten the tail and press on, then return to the oven for 5 hours.

~ *Finger Puppets* ~

These salt dough puppets are simple to construct and could be made by children. The details, such as the giraffe's horns and braided tail, the fox's fur tail and whiskers provide wonderful finishing touches.

6. Undercoat the puppets with acrylic gesso or matt emulsion (flat latex) paint. Leave to dry, then paint with acrylic or craft paints, following the colours in the photograph. After painting a green base to the crocodile, sponge on a thin film of yellow paint for a subtle effect. Finally, when dry, apply 5 layers of satin varnish to the models. To make the giraffe's tail, cut three lengths of stranded cotton embroidery thread. Thread these through the hole and knot the ends inside the puppet. Braid the threads and knot the extending ends together. Fray the ends.

7. To make the fox's tail, use the tail template to cut a shape from fur fabric. Dab glue on the underside and glue on to the salt dough tail.

~ Toys, Games & Animals ~

Nutcracker Soldier

This delightful, old-fashioned toy was a favourite in nineteenth-century Germany. This smart fellow is modelled over a cardboard tube and has movable arms, which are attached to the body with a length of gold cord. Bright acrylic paints give a really attractive finish.

YOU WILL NEED

~

brown paper tape

scissors

ruler

cardboard paper-towel tube

sheet of hardboard (to fit in oven)

cooking fat or vegetable oil

1 quantity salt dough (see page 16)

rolling pin

small, sharp knife

baking parchment
(parchment paper)

skewer

baking tray

baking foil

acrylic gesso or matt emulsion
(flat latex) paint

paintbrushes

acrylic or craft paints

polyurethane satin varnish

scraps of fur fabric

scissors

all-purpose household glue

fine gold cord

large-eyed sewing needle

1. Cut the brown paper tape into lengths. Cut these in half lengthways and stick them over the top of a cardboard paper-towel tube so that the opening is covered. Smear a sheet of hardboard with a generous layer of cooking fat or vegetable oil to prevent the dough from sticking to it. Roll the dough out to an approximate thickness of 5/16 in (8 mm).

2. Place the tube on the hardboard and lay the dough over the top. Tuck the dough around the tube and trim neatly where it meets the board. Trim the top and base. Press a piece of rolled-out dough over the covered end of the tube, and cut the edges level with the dough covering the tube. Pat with a moistened finger to join the dough edges together.

~ Toys, Games & Animals ~

3. From the remaining dough, mould a small triangle for the nose, moisten it and press to the soldier. Mark a vertical division for the legs, then indent the division again with the knife to make it deeper. ▸

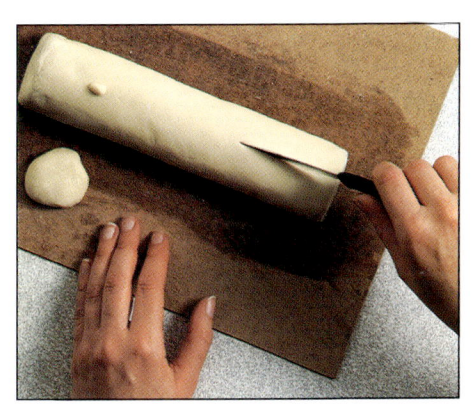

~ *Nutcracker Soldier and Sailor* ~

The soldier's companion, the stocky little sailor, is made in exactly the same way as his taller friend, yet using a shorter inner tube and altering the features.

~ Toys, Games & Animals ~

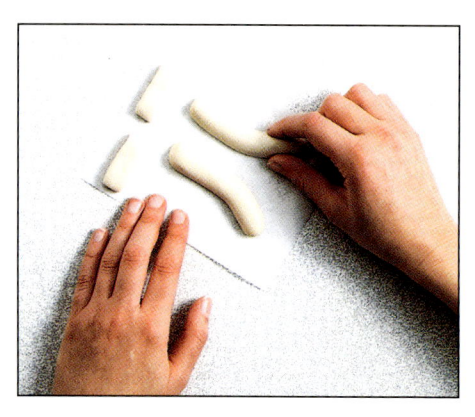

4. Working on baking parchment (parchment paper), roll 2 sausages for the arms, ⅝ in (1.5 cm) thick and 3¼ in (8.5 cm) long. Pat the ends to round them. Flatten the arms slightly and bend each into a curve. To make the feet, roll out a small piece of dough to a thickness of ⅜ in (1 cm), and cut 2 blocks 1 x ⅜ in (2.5 x 1 cm). On each arm, indent the wrists, cuffs and epaulettes with a knife.

5. With a skewer, pierce a hole 3¼ in (8.5 cm) below the top of the soldier on either side for the arms. Pierce a hole through the arms below the epaulettes. Transfer the arms and feet, on the parchment, to a baking tray, and bake all the pieces in the oven at 250°F/120°C/Gas ½ for 6½ hours until the top of the soldier has hardened.

6. Turn the soldier over and support it with baking foil. Roll the dough out flat to a thickness of 5/16 in (8 mm). Cover the back of the model, cutting the edges to fit. Smooth over the joins. Return the model to the oven, and bake all the pieces for a further 4 hours. Standing the soldier upright, butt the feet up against the model. Join to the soldier with a little dough.

7. Return the model to the oven for approximately 1½ hours until hardened, then allow to cool. Undercoat the body and arms with acrylic gesso or matt emulsion (flat latex) paint. Leave to dry, then paint the model in the colours shown. Leave to dry, then apply 5 coats of satin varnish. Cut strips of fur fabric for the hair and beard, cutting through the knitted backing fabric only, then glue in place.

~ *Penguin* ~

This little Arctic creature is made from a solid ball of salt dough; the wings and self-supporting feet are modelled from smaller pieces of dough and added on.

8. Thread the needle with a length of fine gold cord and knot the cord ends tightly together in a double knot. Thread the needle through the hole in one arm, through the soldier's body and then through the other arm. Holding the arms still against the soldier, fasten the cord against the second arm with another double knot. Cut off the excess cord with scissors.

~ Toys, Games & Animals ~

Court Jester

The court jester is a popular theatrical character. This flamboyant joker has a head, hands and legs modelled from baking foil before being covered with salt dough. His fabric body is densely padded and clothed in rich fabrics. The jester's hard, weighty head makes this toy unsuitable for very young children.

YOU WILL NEED
~
baking foil
masking tape
2 small metal bells
baking parchment (parchment paper)
1 quantity salt dough (see page 16)
small, sharp knife
cardboard toilet-roll tube
cooking fat or vegetable oil
baking tray
acrylic gesso or matt emulsion (flat latex) paint
paintbrushes
acrylic or craft paints
polyurethane matt varnish
tracing paper and pencil
scissors
beige, red, blue and black fabric remnants
toy filling (batting)
needle and thread
all-purpose household glue
PVA medium
small gold beads
mohair knitting yarn
gold cord

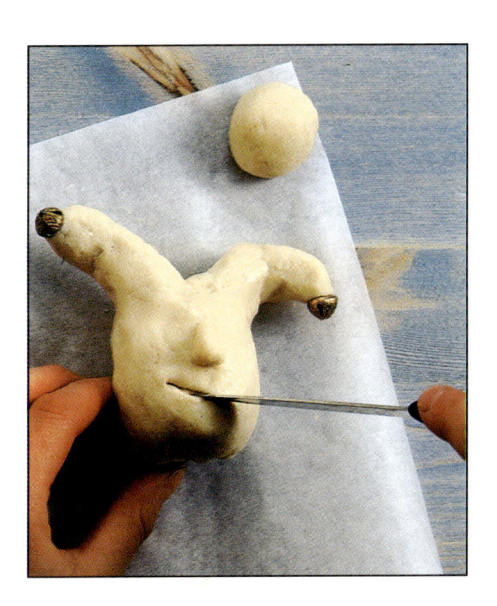

1. Mould an oval of baking foil 2½ in (6 cm) high for the head. Roll 2 sausages of foil, each approximately ¾ in (2 cm) thick and 2 in (5 cm) long, for the hat points. Squeeze one end of each sausage into a point and bend into a curve. Stick the points to the top of the head with short strips of masking tape, and stick a bell to each point, also with masking tape.

2. Working on baking parchment (parchment paper), smear dough over the front of the mould to a thickness of ¼ in (5 mm). Mould a small triangle for the nose, moisten it and press to the face. Roll a ball of dough for the chin, moisten it and press into place. Stroke to blend the chin smoothly to the head. Cut a slit for the mouth, using the tip of a knife. ▶

~ Toys, Games & Animals ~

3. Cut a toilet-roll tube in half lengthwise, and smear one half with cooking fat or vegetable oil. Roll 2 balls of dough 1 in (2.5 cm) in diameter for the hands. Mould these into ovals and flatten them over the toilet-roll tube. Cut into one edge with the tip of a knife to form the thumb, and pat the edges with the knife to round them.

4. Roll 2 sausages of dough and press across the end of each hand. Mould 2 sausages of foil for the legs, each ¾ in (2 cm) thick and 5 in (13 cm) long. Bend one end of each leg forward 1½ in (3.5 cm) to make the foot. Squeeze the end to a point. Smear the top of the leg and foot with dough, moulding the tip of the foot upwards to a point.

5. Transfer all the pieces, on the parchment, to a baking tray, and support the head and legs with baking foil. Bake in the oven at 250°F/120°C/Gas ½ for 4 hours. Allow to cool. Smear the remainder of the head and legs with dough. Remove the hands from the toilet-roll tube and then return all the pieces to the oven for a further 3 hours.

6. Roll 3 balls of dough ⅝ in (1.5 cm) in diameter. Flatten the balls, then press under the base of the head and on to the tops of the legs. Support with baking foil and return to the oven for 6 hours. Leaving the skin tone of the head and hands unpainted, undercoat the model with acrylic gesso or matt emulsion (flat latex) paint. Leave to dry, then paint with acrylic or craft paints, applying a blush of pink to the cheeks. Allow to dry, then apply 5 coats of matt varnish.

~ *Alphabet Fun* ~

This little girl clambering on the letter "S" makes a perfect present. Any letter of the alphabet can be decorated with a brightly coloured figure in this way.

7. Size the body, clothing and mask templates on page 157, transfer to tracing paper, and cut out. Cut out 2 fabric bodies. Mark the broken lines. Taking a ¼ in (5 mm) seam allowance, stitch the pieces together, leaving open the hand and leg ends and the neck between the dots. Stitch the inner-leg seams as far as the cross, then snip the seam allowance around the curves and to the cross. Turn right-side out, and fill the body with toy filling (batting).

~ Toys, Games & Animals ~

8. Stitch along the broken lines through both thicknesses of fabric, then turn under ¼ in (5 mm) at the neck, hand and leg openings. Gather the folded edge of the neck opening with a running stitch. Insert the rim of the head and draw up the thread to gather the fabric tightly around the rim. Dab sparingly with glue and secure the thread. Attach the hands and legs in the same way.

9. Use the templates to draw a blouse and trousers on to the wrong side of beige and red fabric, a scarf on the wrong side of blue fabric and a jester mask on the wrong side of black fabric. Apply PVA medium to the zig-zagged blouse and trouser edges, the outer edges of the scarf and all over the mask (this will help prevent the fabric from fraying). Set aside to dry, then cut out.

10. Stitch the blouse sections together along the centre-front seam, and along the centre-back seam to the dot. Fold the blouse in half with right sides facing. Stitch the side seams, then snip the seam allowance around the curves. Fold the trouser sections in half with right sides facing. Stitch the inner-leg seams, then snip the seam allowance around the curves. Stitch the trousers together along the crotch seam.

11. Turn the blouse and trousers right-side out. Sew small gold beads to the points, and dab PVA medium on to the stitching on the inside to secure in place. Slip on the trousers and sew the upper edge to the body. Put the blouse on to the doll and handsew the centre-back seam. Fold under the neck edge, gather the folded edge and sew to the body. Tie the scarf around the neck and dab on glue sparingly to secure.

12. Gather the blouse and trousers along the broken lines on the pattern. Draw up the threads tightly around the rims of the hands and legs, fasten securely and carefully glue in place. Scrunch up some mohair yarn and glue to the head as hair, and glue the mask in position on the face. Finally, tie a length of gold cord around the waist to form a belt. ▶

~ *Court Jester* ~
(overleaf)

This doll is modelled on the old porcelain figures which had a fabric body and china head and hands. The weight of the jester's head means that the doll lolls in a realistic fashion, particularly fitting for a royal jester whose function was to perform as a buffoon at feasts. The basic doll structure can be adapted with a change of costume to make any manner of dolls, either for gifts or as collectable items.

~ *Toys, Games & Animals* ~

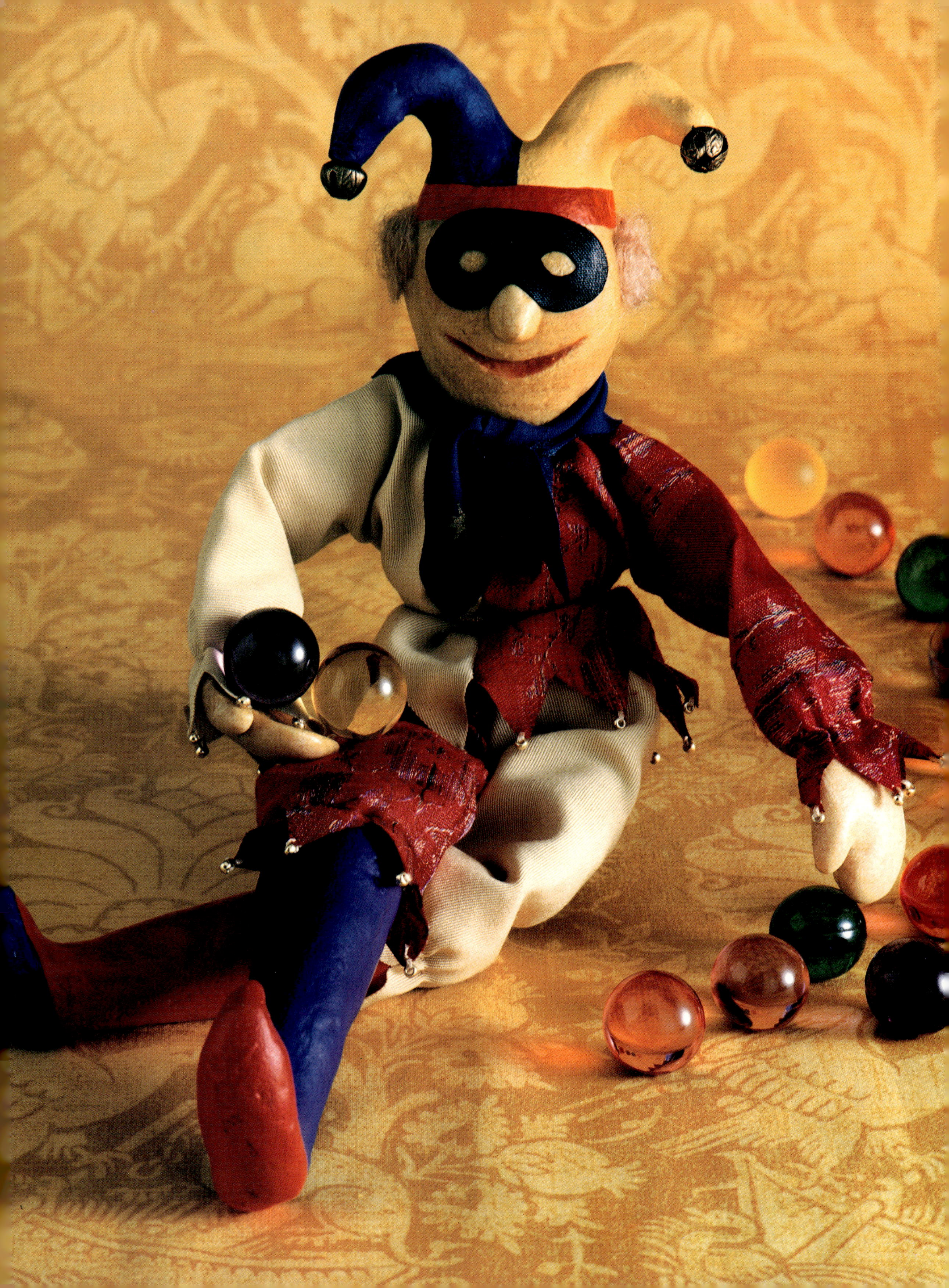

~ Clowns at Play ~

These bright clowns are designed to decorate a wall. They are made as flat-backed plaques with the features added in relief. The facial details are added last, with hair made from dough pushed through a garlic press. The balloons are modelled as separate pieces, and are joined to the clowns using colourful ribbons as string. The balloons can be hung in a variety of positions, giving the impression that they are blowing in the wind.

~ Toys, Games & Animals ~

Templates

Templates are guides which can be traced around in order to transfer a design on to the object to be decorated. In order to enlarge the templates to the size that you require, draw a grid of equal-sized squares over your tracing. Measure the space where the shape is to go and then draw a grid to these proportions, with an equal number of squares as appear on your tracing. Take each square individually and draw the relevant parts of the pattern in the larger square. Alternatively, you can enlarge your tracing on a photocopier if you have access to one and permission to use it.

Tree Plaques, page 25

Window Ornaments, page 28

Fleur-de-Lys

Star

Crown

~ Templates ~

150

Venetian Mask, page 37

Fruit-Filled Cornucopia, page 43

Wheatsheaf Base, page 39

~ *Templates* ~

151

Mexican Box, page 72

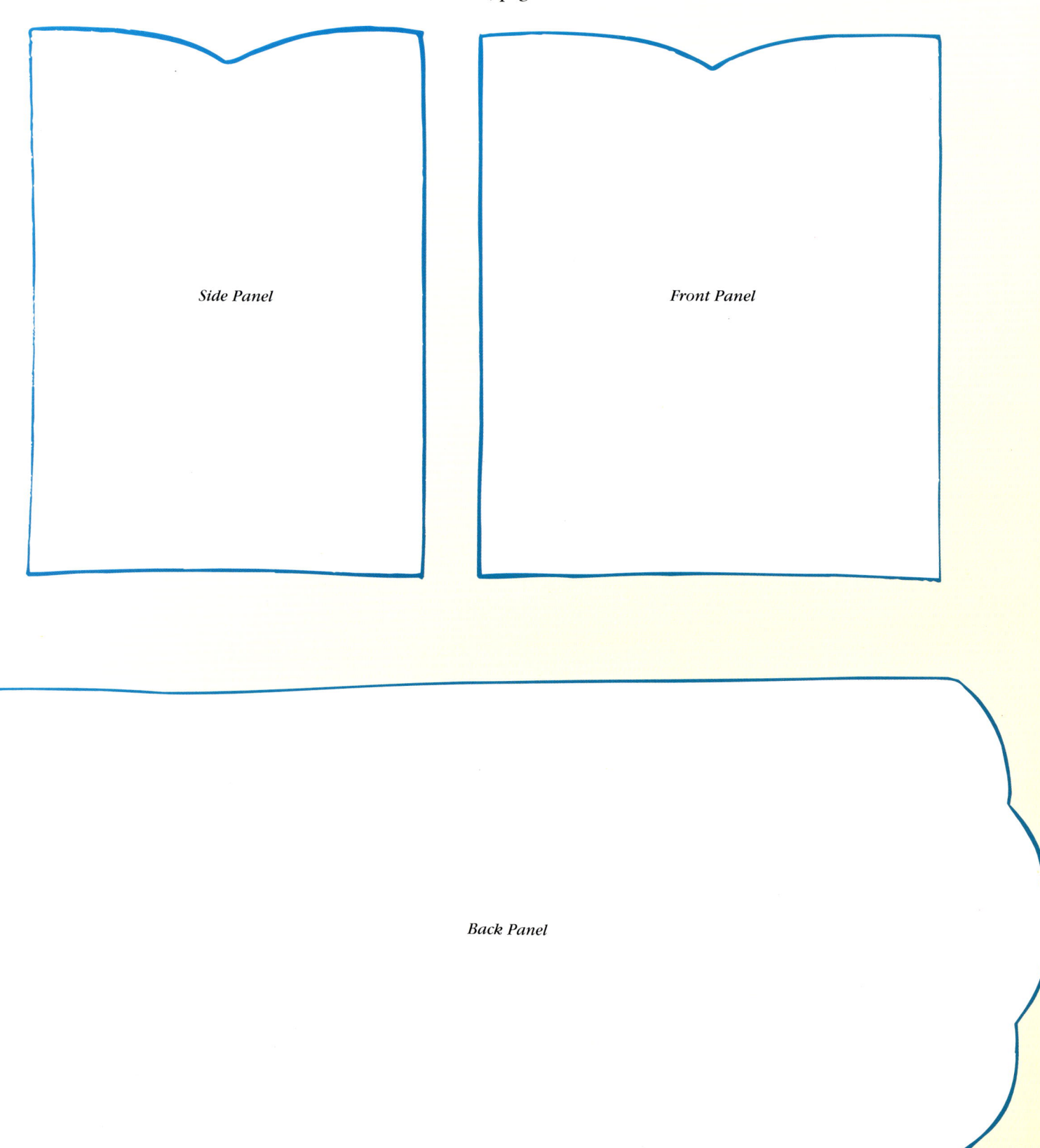

Side Panel

Front Panel

Back Panel

~ Templates ~
152

Elephant and Fish Dishes, page 61

Fish Plaque, page 85

Folk Angel, page 88

Sponged Goose Keyrack, page 99

~ Templates ~

Flying Angel, page 113

Gingerbread Heart, page 108

Checkered Heart, page 110

Sun Plaque, page 103

~ Templates ~

154

Mosaic Mirror, page 117

Mosaic Mirror Stand

~ *Templates* ~

Framed Fish, page 119

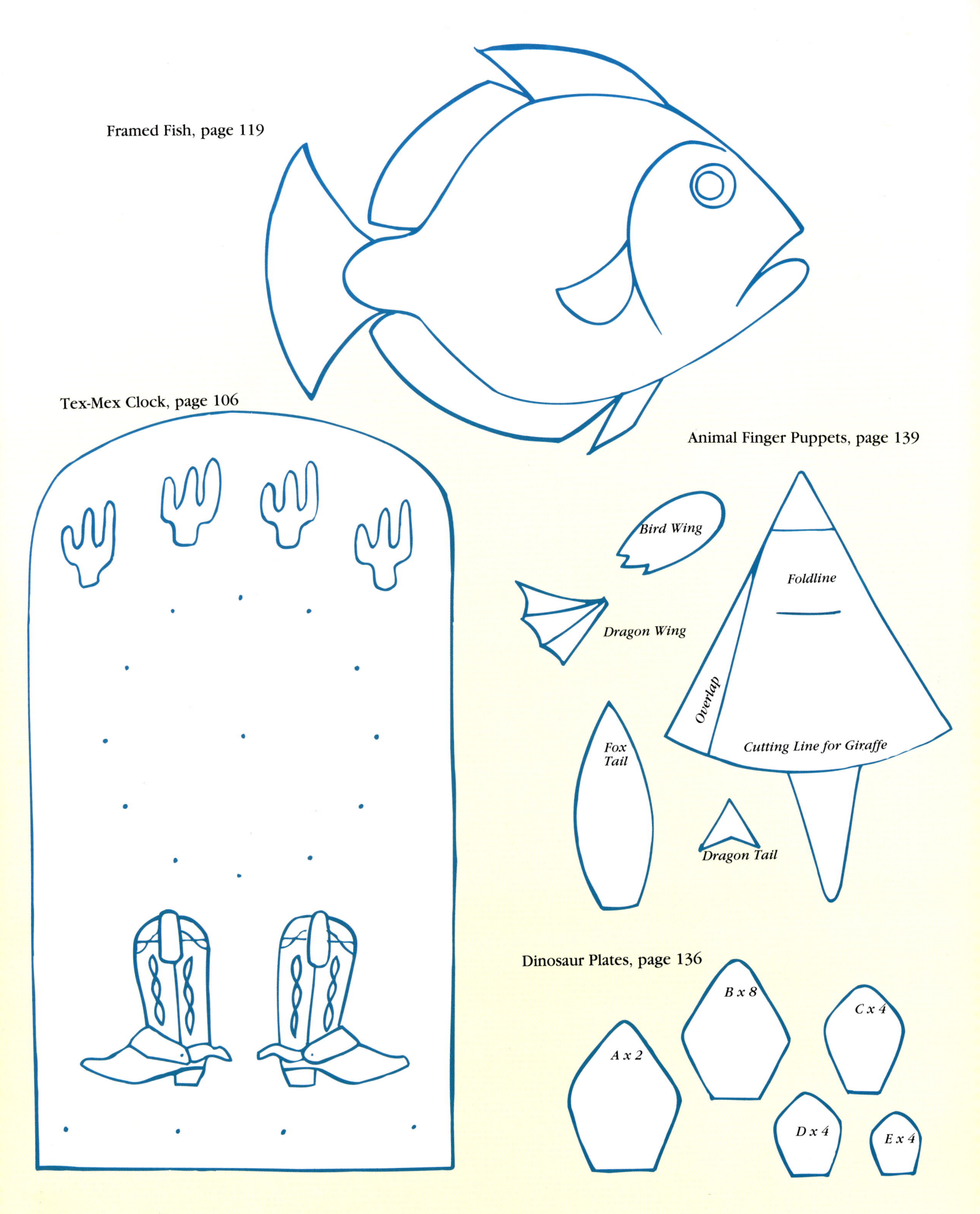

Tex-Mex Clock, page 106

Animal Finger Puppets, page 139

Bird Wing

Dragon Wing

Foldline

Overlap

Fox Tail

Cutting Line for Giraffe

Dragon Tail

Dinosaur Plates, page 136

A x 2

B x 8

C x 4

D x 4

E x 4

~ Templates ~

Body

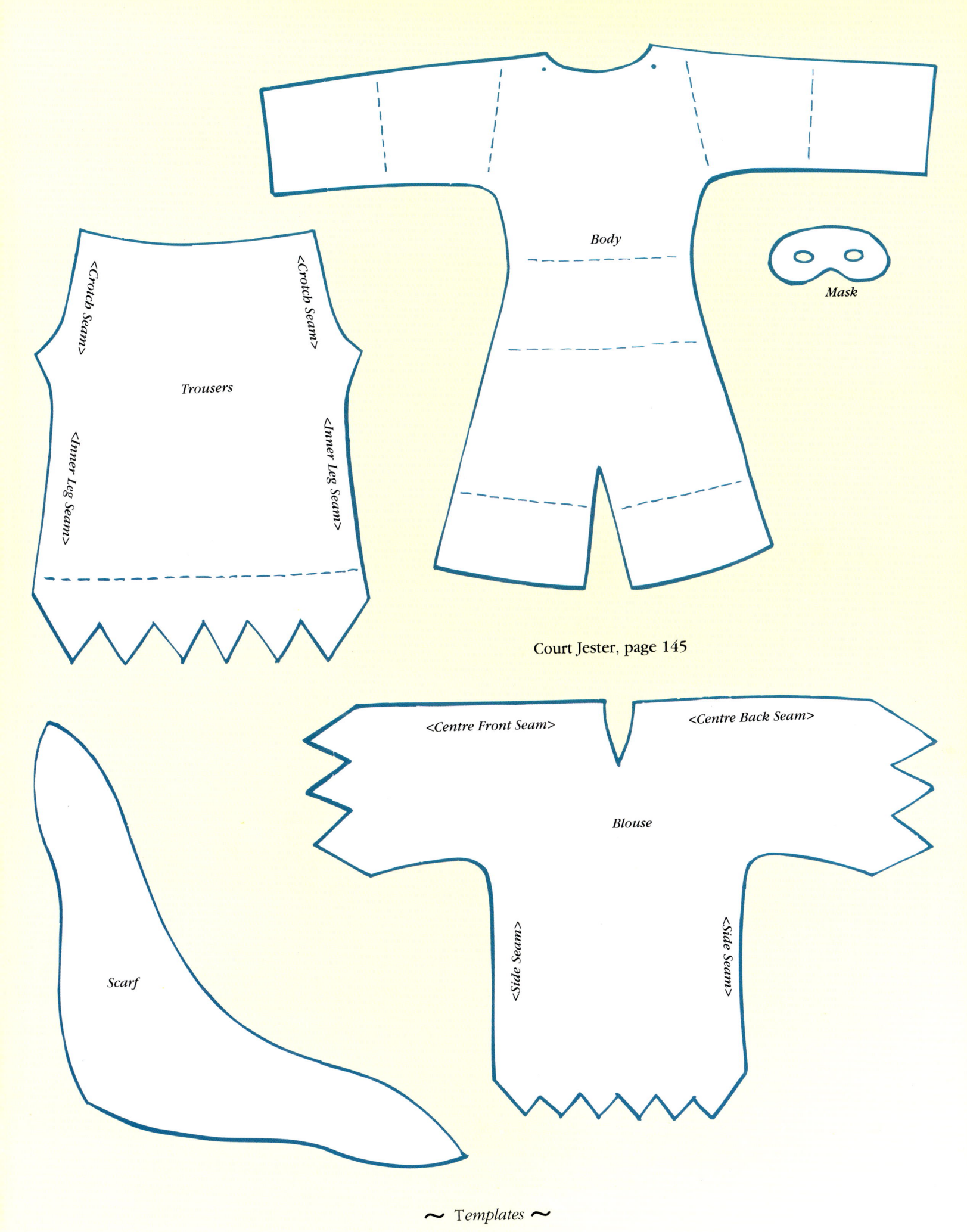

Mask

Trousers
<Crotch Seam>
<Crotch Seam>
<Inner Leg Seam>
<Inner Leg Seam>

Court Jester, page 145

Scarf

Blouse
<Centre Front Seam>
<Centre Back Seam>
<Side Seam>
<Side Seam>

~ Templates ~

157

Index

Air bubbles, 12
Air-drying, 12
Alphabet fun, 146
Angels
  celebration, 115
  flower, 115
  Flying, 113–115
  Folk, 88–90
Animals
  Dinosaur, 136–138
  dough menagerie, 100
  finger puppets, 139–141
  fragile horses, 21
  hanging, 25
  Lion's Head, 91–93
  Tree Plaques, 25–26
  warthog, 138
Armatures
  dinosaur, 19
  making, 19
Autumn leaves, 35

Baking parchment, 11
Basket, spring, 45
Beads
  Bead Necklace, 49–51
  Grapes and Fallen-leaf, 33–35
Boats, Flotilla of, 126–128
Boiled sweets (candies)
  stained-glass effect, creating, 28
Bowls
  Metal-embedded, 63–65
  Needlework Casket, 78–79
  rose, 45
  String and Shell, 66–67
Boxes
  Mexican, 72–74
  Tasselled, 70–71
  Valentine's, 75–77
Bright rings, 50
Brooches
  Classical Collection, 30–32
Burrs, 12

Casket, needlework, 78–79
Celebration angel, 115
Checkered Hearts, 110–112
Checker Board, 133–135
Cherubic head, 90
Chestnut leaves, transfers from, 34
Chickens, Mexican, 74
Children's hands, 94
Christmas tree and wreath, 26

Citrus-fruit plates, 68–69
Classical sources, 32
Clocks
  Tex-Mex, 106–107
  Wall, 122–123
Clowns, garland of, 129–132
Colouring, 11, 17
Container, salt dough as, 73
Cornucopia, fruit-filled, 42–45
Court Jester, 145–148
Crown Letter Rack, 52–53

Decorations
  fleur-de-lys and star, 29
  moulded fish, 62
Dinosaur, 136–138
  armature, 19
Dishes
  Elephant and Fish, 59–62
Dough menagerie, 100

Earrings
  Classical Collection, 30–32
Egyptian head, 12
Elephant and Fish dishes, 59–62
Embedding, 20
Embossing, 20
Equipment, 15

Family of seahorses, 121
Figures, stone-like, 94
Finger puppets, animal, 139–141
Fish
  Fish Plaque, 84–87
  Framed, 119–121
  moulded, 62
Flag-flying tug, 128
Fleur-de-lys, 29
Flotilla of Boats, 126–128
Flower Angel, 115
Flower garland, 38
Flower vase, 80–81
Flowers, making, 48
Flying angel, 113–115

Folk Angel, 88–90
Fragile horses, 21
Framed Fish, 119–121
Fruit-filled Cornucopia, 42–45

Garland
  Clowns, of, 129–132
  flower, 38
Germany
  Christmas tree decorations, 9
Gesso, 14
Gingerbread Heart, 108–109
Goose Keyrack, sponged, 99–101
Grapes and Fallen-Leaf Beads, 33–35

Hands
  Children's, 97
  Indian, 98
  Mexican, 98
  Shaker, 94–97
Hanging animals, 25
Heads
  cherubic, 90
  Egyptian, 12
Hearts
  Chequered, 110–112
  Gingerbread, 108–109
  fabels, 112
  mirror of the heart, 118
Horses, fragile, 21

Indian hand, 98
Inks, 14

Jewellery
  Classical Collection, 30–32

Keyrack, Sponged Goose, 99–101

Labels, heart, 112
Leaves
  autumn, 35
  chestnut, 34
Letter Rack, Crown, 52–53
Lion's head, 91–93

Marbled effects, 71
Marbling, 16
Marine moulds, 11
Masks, Venetian, 35–38
Materials, 15
Metal-embedded bowls, 63–65
Mexican Box, 72–74

Mexican chickens, 74
Mexican Hands, 98
Mexican Tree of Life, 46–48
Mirror, mosaic, 116–118
Mirror of the heart, 118
Modelling knife, using, 11
Modelling techniques
   history of, 9
   surface for, 9
Models
   finishing, 12, 14
   painting, 12, 14, 21
   repairing, 21
   varnishing, 14, 21
Mosaic Mirror, 116–118
Moulded fish, 62
Moulded shells, 67
Moulds
   chocolate-making, used in, 10
   heat-resistance, materials for, 11
   making, 18
   marine, 11

Napkin Rings
   designer patterns, 57
   Spiky, 56–57
Necklace, Bead, 49–51
Needlework Casket, 78–79
Nutcracker Sailor, 143
Nutcracker Soldier, 142–144

Ornaments, window, 28–29

Paint
   acrylic, 14
   craft, 14
   dough, applied on, 12
   gesso, 14
   matt emulsion, 14
   watercolour, 12
Paintbrushes, 14
Painted plate, 21
Pencil holder, 54–55
Penguin, 144
Plaques
   Fish, 84–87
   Sun, 103, 105
   Tree, 25–26
Plates
   Citrus-fruit, 68–69
   painted, 21
Poppies, 40

Rings, bright, 50
Rose bouquet, 10
Rose bowl, 45

Sailor, Nutcracker, 143
Salt dough
   baking, 12, 20
   colouring, 11, 16
   container, as, 73
   craft medium, as, 9
   decorating, 21
   embedding, 20
   embossing, 20
   making, 10
   marbling, 16
   protecting, 21
   raw, 16
   recipe, 16
   rolling out, 11, 16
   steam, keeping away from, 73
   storing, 10
   textures, 12
   water and flour, using, 11
   working with, 11
Seahorses, family of, 121
Shaker Hand, 94–97
Shells
   moulded, 67
   moulds, as, 86
Shooting stars, 90
Soldier, Nutcracker, 142–144
Spiky Napkin Rings, 56–57
Sponged Goose Keyrack, 99–101
Spring basket, 45
Stained-glass effect, 28
Star, 29
Starfish, 86
Stick-pins
   Classical Collection, 30–32
String and Shell Bowls, 66–67
Structures, 19
Sun
   classical motif, 32
   Plaque, 103–105
Sun and moon, 105

Tasselled Boxes, 70–71
Templates, 150–157
   using, 11, 18
Tex-Mex clock, 106–107
Textures, 12
Transfers
   leaves, from, 34
Tree
   Christmas, 26
   plaques, 25–26
Tree of life, Mexican, 46–48
Tug, flag-flying, 128

Valentine's boxes, 75–77
Varnishing, 14, 21
Vase, flower, 80–81
Vase of flowers, 48
Venetian Masks, 35–38

Wall Clock, 122–123
Warthog, 138
Wheatsheaf, 39–41
Window ornaments, 28–29
Wreath, Christmas, 26

~ Index ~

Acknowledgements

The author and publishers would like to thank the following for their help in compiling this book:
British Alcan Consumer Products Ltd, Amersham, Bucks, UK, for providing baking foil and baking parchment paper
Cuprinol Ltd, Frome, Somerset, UK, for providing water-based varnishes.

They would also like to thank the following artists for their tremendous contributions:
Petra Boase: pages 50, 51, 53, 55, 57, 67, 76, 77, 81, 123,
Lucinda Ganderton: pages 12 (top), 41, 42, 46, 90 (bottom), 98 (top & bottom), 100, 101, 105 (bottom), 109, 111, 112 (top & bottom), 114, 115, 118, 160.
Ariane Gastambide: page 78.
Carol Pastor: pages 6 (left), 10, 11, 12 (bottom), 34, 62, 86, 87, 90 (top).
Bee Smithwick: pages 7 (all models), 13, 21, 26, 38, 40, 44, 45, 48, 121, 144, 146, 149.
Dorothy Wood: pages 6 (right), 64, 104.